God and Utopia

Gabriel Vahanian

GOD AND UTOPIA

THE CHURCH
IN A TECHNOLOGICAL
CIVILIZATION

A Crossroad Book · *The Seabury Press* · New York

1977 · *The Seabury Press*
815 Second Avenue · New York, N.Y. 10017

Published originally under the title
Dieu et l'utopie, l'Eglise et la technique
© 1976, Les Editions du Cerf, Paris

Translated by Paul Lachance, O.F.M., Paul Schwartz,
Roman Duncan Kozak, and the author.

Printed in the United States of America

Library of Congress Cataloging in Publication Data

Vahanian, Gabriel, 1927–   God and utopia.
"A Crossroad book."
Translation of Dieu et l'utopie.
1. Christianity—20th century. 2. Technology and
ethics. 3. Utopias—Religious aspects. 4. Eschatology.
I. Title.
BR121.2.V2613   261   77-24029   ISBN 0-8164-0355-4

Pour Noëlle

Contents

Preface

From the death of God to the death of man there was but a short step. And it was taken rather quickly.

But has it been to the detriment of the Christian faith?

Certainly, at least in the short run. The secularization of Christianity, no longer peripheral, now affects more than merely minor and external (though religious) questions relating to the preambles of faith. In the past, whatever role was assigned to God, whatever image one had of him (grand architect or master watchmaker), Christianity was always able to accommodate itself. Ironic as this might now appear, it could even rely upon a religiosity whose tenacity had in fact outlasted its usefulness. But today secularization attacks the very heart of faith. The church is emptying, even as those who remain seek comfort in its ancient visage as the people of God.

The world has moved. And rightly or wrongly exposed the illusory character of the religious scaffolding which previously held it in place.

Yet it remains to be seen whether the cultural shift thus initiated must result necessarily in the obliteration, the final occlusion of Christianity, or simply in its temporary eclipse. Without minimizing the present deficiencies of the Christian faith, we must note that nothing would be more imprudent than to insist on relegating theology to the ranks of the obsolete sciences, alongside Ptolemaic astronomy or pre-Columbian geography. Challenging every absolutism used to dress up gods (or, for that matter, men), theology unmasks the tyranny of false assurances and deceptive hopes nourished by religion. It denounces the despotism underlying all disfigurations of man. Indeed, to the extent that it speaks of God, theology sides with man—by taking sides for his future. It sides precisely with the man whose death our celebrated thinkers proclaim, a man who worships no gods but those that die, a man who—like Moses struck dead on the threshhold of the promised land—has learned to master nature only to run the risk of being banished from it.

To be sure, we must not confuse theology with its cultural envelope,[1] nor ecology with naturism or even naturalism, nor the development of the human project with the messages of various false prophets of history. Man with his gift of freedom always gives the impression of being a surd when seen from a historical perspective; from a purely natural viewpoint he appears stillborn. Whatever the circumstances, theology is concerned with man. And just as our heritage implies a natural theology, it also implies a theology of history. But the man with whom theology is at present concerned is no longer confronted with the deficiencies of a nature which would put man himself into question, but is faced with balancing the ecological relations without which nature itself would be called into question. Nor is this man confronted with the decrees of a history which will reject him if he does not somehow or other adhere to them in the hope of discovering in them the pattern of a project worthy of him and suited to his destiny. Rather, the man with whom theology is concerned today is man confronting the fabrications of technology.

Such a man is no longer prey to a disfiguring scarcity, but to abundance—though a deceptive abundance. As a result of this abundance, wealth increases while poverty is checked—though not eliminated. Never has abundance been so aware of its own contradiction, its futility.

Faced with the achievements of technology, man accepts such abundance. But he accepts it with resignation.

Showered with riches, Job remains Job. And man remains in hope—but a hope which nothing gratifies or annihilates, since man is still imperfect: he is yet to be realized. Nothing can blunt

---

1. Theology may be implicated in the decay of a particular form of Western civilization; however, "doing" theology need not be confused with doing the autopsy of a civilization.

the utopianism which, in the computer age as in the barely forgotten days of the natural "order of things," constitutes what is proper to man. It is true that from one age to the next cultural changes reach such an intensity that at times our minds are befuddled. And shaken as we are by the shameless utopianism which has succeeded the more muted utopianism of the past, we fear for man. Simply because he is losing or merely rescinding what we were accustomed to call his "nature," we presume man himself to be doomed, and forget the utopianism which is the distinctive mark of all human reality.

Somehow it was in view of this very utopianism—muted or not—that in the Middle Ages an incipient ideology raised theology to the rank of queen of the sciences, while at the same time implicating science itself in the quest for that utopia which was defined as the beatific vision of God, as the future life. With such definitions, theology was ultimately bound to capitulate to its own scholasticism, whether Catholic or Protestant, and turn into a system, unable to conceive of utopia except in terms of scarcity: a scarcity which no doubt meant in the beginning merely a failure of goods and services but in the end meant a "failure of nerve," a failure of the distinctively "human." For its part, science has done no better than theology. In its arrogance, science collapses into naturalism. Under the cover of the laws of nature, it stages its own comeback by colonializing man and turning him away from the utopianism through which he controls and exercises his right *to* the world.

Today, in the wake of the triumph of technology, what we are witnessing is precisely the resurgence of true utopianism. In contrast with the pseudo-theology of scholasticism, technology makes no appeal whatsoever to any notion of scarcity in seeking a foundation for utopianism. In contrast with science, which likewise seeks to cancel out faith by binding man to some sham "order of things," technology releases man's religious drive. Indeed, the technological problem, first and foremost, is a religious problem, with the difference that now "the religious" is no longer defined in terms of shortage—material or, for that matter, human—but in terms of abundance. Religion is no longer linked to hominization, but to humanization. And the human, no longer consigned to the outskirts of utopia, now provides the utopian drive with its proper focus.

By way of simple illustration, one may note that there is hardly anything less utopian than Robinson Crusoe and his soothing picture of nature at once benevolent and indulgent. Barely, if at all, does Crusoe differ from Ivan Karamazov, who simply hands his ticket back to God. Returning to nature, Crusoe becomes a sort of robot: the human dehumanized, the exploiter exploited, that against which even Ivan rebels with all his strength. From Crusoe's perspective man is reduced to a datum of nature, while for Ivan he is at least something to be realized. For Crusoe, abundance is a matter of inserting man into nature and of domesticating it eventually. In contrast, Ivan is concerned with the integration of man. The former has done nothing but dethrone theology; consequently, for him all is grace. The latter wonders how man can be something if God is nothing, how everything can be grace if God must die. He heralds a new religious vision,[2] the very one which, through technology, is now challenging theology.

At the dawn of the technological era, it would obviously be foolish to deny that theology is culturally insolvent, deaf, and dumb. It would be foolish also to deny that such a cultural insolvency, accentuated by both religious fatigue and spiritual erosion, is what hampers theology and locks it up in ecclesiastic institutions stubbornly tangled in the inertia of centuries. Yet this locking of theology both on the religious level (fatigue or erosion) and on the cultural level (insolvency) does more harm to the church than does the vigorous secularism of its disillusioned clergy who rightly yearn for a faith without frontiers, for a God with a human face.

Furthermore, in the midst of a civilization not even interested in liquidating its interest in the Christian faith, it would be no less foolish to deny that this theology tends to collapse the moment it seeks to make itself heard—were the church even to listen to it. In fact, more often than not, the church distrusts theology as it does all things that happen *extra muros* and that

---

2. *Religiosité* is the term rendered either by "religious vision," or by "religious sensibility," or simply by "religiosity."

are, by the same token, banished *extra ecclesiam*. Of course, what does it really matter if theology is denied ecclesiastical sanction? Is not the main thing that theology should know how to steer clear of every jurisdiction which would enslave it to one ideology or another?

A theology exclusively geared to the church would only be justified by a church severed from the world. Indeed, nothing has been more harmful to the understanding of faith than the now "classic" distinction between a theology for internal use and a theology for external use, between dogmatics and apologetics. Such a split has only succeeded in aggravating the cleavage between church and world, a *cleavage* which diverts theology from its object, since by its nature theology must extend beyond the borders of the church, if only because faith is in a sense inconceivable except in relation to unbelief; a *cleavage*, too, which compels theology to emigrate. Traces of this can be seen in the way in which theology attacks those very ideologies which —because they pride themselves on having dispossessed Christianity—imagine themselves to be the unique achievements of contemporary thought.

Admittedly, Christianity today seems to have dried up at its source. It does not quench the thirst for spiritual instauration and for social and cultural iconoclasm after which the contemporary world yearns. And its impotence is even more alarming when it is overwhelmed by the automatization of nature or the robotization of ethics. What kind of a man will ever emerge from a test tube when ethics and religion are both put under a bushel? What kind of a man, indeed, if not a man no more atheist than theist?

In this regard, at least outside the church, few people are deceived; these are the people for whom the collapse of theism implies the collapse of atheism as well; people for whom the collapse of theism is truly complete only when it implicates atheism; people for whom technology concerns man precisely insofar as he lies beyond this traditional opposition of theism and atheism—on the very horizon of a true theology. And this is a theology which, though harassed and denounced by believers, still fascinates a good number of unbelievers, attracting particularly those for whom atheism, by becoming an ideology, has also collapsed.[3] A curious patient, indeed, who whispers to the doctor what diagnosis he must make.

Disenchanted with atheism on the one hand, and prodded by technology on the other, a religious sensibility with different contours appeals to modern man—different, and also new in the sense that it remains sensitive to transcendence without thereby falling into the dualistic trap in which the sacred is opposed to the profane. Transcendence is affirmed, not as a function of something alien to man, of something lacking in man, but as a function of that which man does not lack when he is fully man: namely, "God." Transcendence is affirmed and, accordingly, grasped as the expression of the utopianism inherent in the human reality in its integrity. As I have said, this of course in no way attenuates the present sclerosis of Christianity. But neither can it be denied that this makes more plausible the aptitude of the heart, once transplanted, to nurture the organism that will know better than to reject it: it makes plausible the aptitude of Christianity to tap the human potential of technology. Given the role of Christianity in the flowering of technology, it is logical, at the very least, to point out their affinities. The Greco-Roman world certainly did not exhibit such affinities to Christian faith, and yet allowed it to flourish. If early Christianity could adapt itself to the constraints of a natural religion, what prevents it now from adopting the framework of a religious sensibility determined by technology?

Accordingly, *either* Christianity will entrench itself in a cultural ghetto preserved by a church with outdated structures, and theology will cease to hinge church and world (there would be nothing left for it but to file a petition for bankruptcy), *or*—since God rests more easily in man's hope than in nature—Christianity can abandon the sterile attitude it has displayed for too long a time, an attitude which consists in regarding science and technology as blighted, and can with all its breath fan man's desire for the human—on which even technology subsists—by preventing him from falling into the chaos of nature, a nature from which technology itself issues, even as it is only through

---

3. Cf. F. Fonvieille-Alquier, *La fin des dogmatismes* (Calmann-Lévy, Paris, 1973).

technology that nature is brought to consciousness. Thus the human consists less in conforming to nature than in releasing nature's own utopianism, in bringing it into conformity not simply with *man,* himself a product of nature, but with *the human,* with precisely that which it is nature's own mission to honor, if only because nature itself is not excluded from it. Nor is it inappropriate to recall here that for classical theology, nothing stands in need of salvation more than natural man. Natural man is inauthentic man. Doubtless, nature can also symbolize renewal; but it symbolizes decay no less sharply. Doomed to corruption, only through grace does nature become natural.

No doubt some might affirm that theology despises nature. But they will have understood neither. It is simply a question of realizing that whenever nature reasserts itself, as in senescence, it only succeeds in propping up the inhuman. In contrast to nature—presumably representing God knows what fountain of youth—theology at least has the merit of refusing to lock itself into the smug optimism of any naturism. To be convinced of this, one need only scan the mythological symbolism of salvation itself: it is in the "other world" that natural man, pardoned and "reconverted" to his true nature, is able at last to enjoy nature fully. I should have said: in a *new* world. Without denying what compromises such a conception of salvation entails, it has at least the advantage of not sinking into naturism, much less of mistaking it for some distant vestige of paradise.

Moreover, that advantage is also that of the utopianism (inherited almost exclusively from such a Christianity) which furnishes technology with its essential characteristic, basing it on the permanent transformation of the world—in a word, on the *novum.* Here again, technology is the heir of theology and its critique of the idea of nature. This critique is based on the eschatological notion of salvation (new life and new world), according to which there can be no salvation except where God reigns, where "the heavens answer for the earth," where "the earth answers for the corn, the new wine and the oil" (Hos. 2:22), and "gives of its fruits" (Ps. 67:6) for "the earth is the Lord's and everything in it" (Deut. 10:14; 1 Cor. 10:26).

From myth to technique, from the sacred to utopia, the problematic of the Christian faith has at least maintained a constant character. It remains centered on the church as a principle of social transformation, of political involvement, or of cultural iconoclasm. Whatever the response to this problematic—from "beatific vision" of God to "future life" by way of the God who reigns—it issues from a single principle: the eschatological utopianism of faith whose iconoclasm opens up, not on the negation of the world, but on its transformation; in other words, on an ecclesial revolution of society, whether agrarian or technological.

From this point of view, Chapter I constitutes not only a kind of retrospective of Christianity, especially Western Christianity as displayed by Saint Augustine, Saint Thomas, and the reformers; but this chapter is also prospective: by comparing salvation and the reign of God, mythology and technology, it seeks to show how the emerging technological phenomenon relates to both the utopian dimension essentially proper to the human reality and to the eschatolgical understanding of faith, the understanding of faith as "eschatic" existence (in the light of which man is man only insofar as he is new man).

Having thus shown how eschatology constitutes the principal dimension of the Christian faith, we consider this problematic in Chapter II from the twofold perspective of ideology and utopia. First, from the perspective of ideology: if only because, on the one hand, the term itself most meaningfully designates everything which today opposes traditional beliefs—to the point of displacing them in the sphere of the psyche no less than in the sphere of daily involvement in the routine of life—and because, on the other hand, Christianity, to the extent that it has promoted institutions, whether ecclesiastic or dogmatic, now plays the role of an ideology. Second, from the perspective of utopia: if only because the term itself is what best characterizes technological civilization, and because Christianity—unable to conceive of the human reality except in the light of the *eschaton* —cannot come to terms with its own understanding of man except, as it did from the very beginning, in terms of utopia. All the more does one need, therefore, to distinguish eschatology from ideology as well as from utopia; differing from ideology, which inevitably drifts into apocalypticism, and differing from utopia, which even under conditions of abundance bears the mark of asceticism in relation to nature (if not to the body), eschatology is by contrast centered on plenitude, on the "fullness of time."

The question with which we must then deal in Chapter III is whether the mutual commitment between man and the human is to be annulled inasmuch as the human can only resign itself to being man, or whether man is bound to go beyond himself in becoming human. Man is, indeed, more than a link in the ecological chain. Indeed, it is by breaking with nature that man becomes man, just as it is by breaking with Adam that the old man becomes a new creature in Christ.

This break does not imply that the human must repudiate man, any more than Christ, the second Adam, repudiates the first Adam. Nor does it imply that there is no limit to man. It implies, however, that what constitutes man's horizon is not nature but the human. The human is that which limits man, and the human is something more than the result of an anthropological, let alone ontological, Darwinism. The human is a utopia of man. The myth of progress, which has nothing to do with utopia, has even less to do with eschatology. And, moreover, inasmuch as it is the human and not nature which constitutes the horizon of man (which is what we mean by "the utopianism of the human reality"), in Christ who is man's ultimate horizon *(eschaton),* the human is also its prolepsis *(novum).* That man remains to be realized—inasmuch as he can only start from scratch—is what in the end is at stake in the dialectic between *eschaton* and *novum.*

From this point of view, Chapter IV takes up the comparison of eschatology and utopia once again, but now focuses on technological utopianism. The argument consists of bringing to light the mutual affinities which unite faith (eschatic existence) and technology (utopian existence). Basically, if eschatology deals with man in Christ—man come to terms with God, that is, with the condition proper to man—then utopia (whose meaning and significance become manifest only through a "technique" of the human) does not throw man back into nature or into history, but reflects at last man come to terms with the human, God's very condition.

Hence, we move on to Chapter V where we consider the

ecclesial utopianism of faith in relation to the utopianism of the human reality as we have described it. In this context we are dealing with the kind of utopianism which was formerly channeled through meditations on the soul or through speculations on the spirit. Today's utopianism is channeled through a "technique" of the body, the body being the index par excellence of the technological understanding of man. But the body is also the index of the church inasmuch as the church, as the body of Christ, finds its meaning as the kingdom at work.

The last chapter is an attempt to define more precisely what must be understood by the notion of church, especially taking into account that the church must come to terms with the exigencies and requirements inherent in the presuppositions of technological civilization.

Humanly speaking, the future of the church lies with technology. But equally, the future of technology requires an ecclesial revolution.

Acknowledgments

However joyful an occasion the publication of a book may be it is also one of thanksgiving. Writing is like contracting debts.

Indebted to Syracuse University, I gratefully acknowledge the support I have constantly received from my students as well as my colleagues, and in particular from Professor Donald E. Kibbey, Vice-President for Research and Graduate Affairs, whose unfailing generosity has helped me carry out this project at each one of its stages, in each aspect of its production, oral or written.

I wish also to express my thanks to Paul Lachance, O.F.M., and Paul Schwartz for providing me with a draft of the English version. Without this draft, as well as a previous version, prepared by Worthington Campbell, and the insightful corrections suggested by Michael S. Kogan, I would not have had the courage to enlist the help of my student, Roman Duncan Kozak, in approving this edition.

Finally, I am grateful to Justus George Lawler: his discriminating sense for language, his friendly but irresistible suggestions or corrections, and his moral commitment to this work have greatly facilitated my task throughout the last few years.

GABRIEL VAHANIAN

Note

I hope the reader will indulge the author's habit, acquired in the course of this work, of defining some categories en route, while their meaning is unfolding or as the argument is drawing to a conclusion. The reason for this is simple enough: it has been difficult to denounce antiquated notions and at the same time marshal these reflections under the aegis of traditional thought. Language carries a price and, were it not paid, the bewilderment of the reader would only be greater. As it is, the reader is not burdened by anything other than the text he is reading, and he need only call upon his own memory if he wants to share the hope of the author.

Nevertheless, some kind of preliminary clarification will be helpful in indicating the perspective from which certain terms come into their own throughout this volume, particularly those terms which have passed over from a mythological system of thought to a technological one.

First, language, whether taken as a system of communication or indifferently as a manifest of the human reality, traces every type of utopianism whereby man becomes truly human. Banal as it might seem, language is composed of words; it therefore has no choice but to assume the totality of their respective etymological load. For example, the word "God" has evoked Zeus as well as Yahweh. But neither the ancient follower of Zeus nor the biblical worshiper of Yahweh would ever be able, mentally or emotionally, to grasp what such a word means today to a man on the threshold of the technological era, whether he is still a partisan of "God" or, supposedly, already much too mature even to be bothered with him.

Conversely, in spite of all appearances, Jean Anouilh's *Antigone* and Jean Paul Sartre's *The Trojans* are plays that insert us into our own time; they are something more than exclusively

Greek tragedies. In fact, the less we identify with the Greeks of old, the more do such plays become relevant to our own self-understanding. Such plays do not return us to the past; they do not hark back to some privileged moment of man's evolution, but have it weigh on us as well as wait on us here and now.

The reason is that language accounts for the etymology of each of its words. But in order to do so without wasting away or smothering itself, it liberates the words from that very etymology and opens them up to new meanings, meanings all the more consistent with the terminology that bore them because they have been weaned on it. True, language does not lock out the past, any more than it gets locked up in it. Language locks into the future: to speak is to hope. Language means migration; it is a pilgrimage. Not a transgression, but a progression: all language is prophetic.

The second remark deals with the Christian faith.

While a common error consists of subjecting Christianity to theism, another error is committed by those, though still relatively few, who succumb to the fascination of reducing it to atheism. Indeed, the Christian faith lies beyond theism as well as beyond atheism; and when it is shut up within theism or within atheism, it is severed from language. Shorn of this utopian dimension, it finally sinks into a system, rationalizing its own caricature as well as divesting itself of all eschatological content. We said above that no language speaks unless it yields to new meaning. Likewise, dead is the faith which, in response to the reality of the new man, does not yield new schemas of the human.

In confessing God, faith not only contests atheism or theism; it also shows that it is infinitely nearer to utopia than to ideology, more at ease with contestation or dissent than with the status quo. It is centered on the reign of God, and this is what we mean to spell out when we say that it is essentially eschatological. One need not, accordingly, reduce faith to a system or to an ideology of instant knowledge or automatic good behavior.

As a result of these two sets of observations, the following additional comment must be made. Though salvation and the reign of God are deliberately contrasted, there is no need to overemphasize the point by having eschatology wholly excluded from the domain of soteriology or, reciprocally, soteriology from the domain of eschatology. Against the background of a technological civilization whose main characteristic is utopianism—and its main drawback perpetual novelty—it is necessary to stress that the Christian faith would be completely disarmed if it could not survive except by conforming to a soteriological model based on the agrarian civilization of a golden age—and its main drawback, the notion of the "good old days," the "sacred time" of the origins. In fact, the specifically eschatological orientation of faith would be blinded. We should note instead that, even in its soteriological phase, Christianity would never cease from associating, for better or for worse, salvation and the reign of God. Nor could it resist the confusion of eschatology (the time of the end) with apocalypse (the end of time)—even though, driven by its doctrine of salvation, it would tend to mistake the inauguration of the reign of God for the end of time.

Finally, the way in which *eschaton* and *novum* are used deserves a mention, and then I will feel that I have perhaps justified the key terms—heirlooms as well as impedimenta—used in this volume.

To parody a famous saying, *eschaton* and *novum* are not words one goes looking for. One discovers them. Perhaps I should have found others that are not so much patchwork as these seem to be, at least at first glance. Convinced, however, that they only seem so, I did not think I should resist a professional habit of appealing to certain technical terms as long as they still had—and only if they still had—some chance of being successfully transplanted, of *taking hold*. Generally speaking, such terms must be considered grafts. Some of them have taken. For example: libido, charismatic, eros, agape, kerygma, cybernetic, and so forth; they read easily enough. Not without risk, of course; but the risk must be taken.

Besides, *eschaton* and *novum* are used in a way which is so restrained as to be quite moderate. *Eschaton* is a Greek word: it means the last, the ultimate in view of which everything else that pretends to be ultimate is challenged and contested. *Novum,* on the other hand, is a Latin word meaning the last in the sense of the most recent, the newest; it can just as easily point to some genuine innovation as it can to the latest novelty ("newest is best"). If the first term evokes destiny, the second hints that this very destiny is to be improvised in faith (as condition of the *novum*) and, likewise, in that charity (as fullness of time) which is accomplished in transcending their dialectic, and so opening God himself to the human and man to the divine. The only difficulty comes, perhaps, from the fact that *eschaton* and *novum* shrink from ever appearing as personifications. Instead, they describe modes of being, or even qualify relations between man and the world, God and man, as well as the manner in which each articulates the other.

Glossary

Apocalypse,
apocalyptic: from a Greek word meaning revelation: taken
                    here in the pejorative sense of some more or
                    less ideological doctrine concerning the end of
                    time, the final catastrophe

Eschatology: from the Greek *eschaton:* ultimate, last—conse-
                    quently, that which is concerned with the time
                    of the end when *God* will be all in all

God: the radically other to whose reality man attests
                    by attesting the very integrity of his own reality

Ideology: a critique of uncritically endorsed ideas, itself
                    become likewise endorsed

Incarnation: that which God is as the radically other whose
                    condition is man

Kingdom,
reign of God: neither the "beyond" nor the end of history;
                    neither a world above nor another world, but
                    an *other* world

Man: a hope of man

Myth: not that which is opposed to science (since
                    technology is their common denominator), but
                    that from which technique takes over (so that
                    science—or religion—is their common denom-
                    inator)

Novum: a Latin word which means new, newness, latest,
                    recent, the last

Pleroma:	from a Greek word meaning fullness as opposed to totality, universality, or plurality as well as uniformity: when *God* is all in all
Religiosity:	not a pejorative, but the fullness of religious sensibility
Technique:	from the Greek *technè:* art, as in art of living; considered as technology (the application of science), technique is part of the mythological universe. On the other hand, in the technological universe, technique consists of a method, of an art of living more than particular applications of science. In changing its universe, technology has changed the universe. From a tool, it has become a method, a "technique of the human," endowed even with its own religious sensibility. Until very recently, usage still limited technology to the applications of science. Nowadays technology—or technique—spells out a mode of being and ultimately a new—technological—phenomenon of man, inasmuch as these applications now affect him in his whole being. While the French language still distinguishes between the terms technology and technique, reserving the latter for this new phenomenon, English simply takes up all the various shades of meaning under one and the same term, technology.
Utopia:	a word coined by Thomas More from the Greek *outopos*, "nowhere"; pointing to what could take place only where, precisely, it has no place. The reality thus designated precedes the word, which dates from the sixteenth century; in fact, utopia constitutes one of the oldest political and social forms of contestation, of responsible dissent.

God and Utopia

I

Christianity's Obsolescence or the Ecclesial Revolution?

1. FROM A CIVILIZATION OF SALVATION TO A CIVILIZATION OF THE REIGN OF GOD

Christianity is not facing its first crisis today. It has gone through many others in twenty centuries. Yet, there is no doubt that the crisis it faces today is its most acute, by far its most severe. In a sense, it is even without precedent. Indeed, this crisis is not only a religious crisis, as we might be tempted to think. It is both religious and cultural.

A. Salvation and the Reign of God, or "Like God, Like Man"

Every cultural complex carries with it its own religiosity. Reciprocally, every religious constellation implies a framework of particular cultural structures. Having left behind the universe of myth for that of technique, contemporary man, bewildered, exposes himself to the constraints of a twofold change: the change is religious to the extent that Christianity, though once deeply involved in a civilization now moribund, is nonetheless implicated in the rise of the technological phenomenon. The change is cultural to the extent that the technological phenomenon, though bound up with Christianity, nonetheless appears to constitute the ultimate negation of the very civilization through which Christianity reached an apogee of sorts.

It is in virtue of this twofold change that we must attempt to understand the technological phenomenon. Accordingly, the quest for cultural identity, if it is to be consistent with the technological phenomenon as a whole, must, to the extent that such a phenomenon is expressive of a particular religiosity, ultimately also involve Christianity. The task itself is such that it entails the responsibility of Christianity in an inalienable—if perhaps partial—manner. Whether partial or not, as a matter of fact it is for this reason that today Christianity is tempted to assume this responsibility even at the price of its own identity, and to the point of losing sight of that which is at stake in the current crisis. Indeed, what will remain of the Christian faith if, under the pretext of living up to the secularity it calls for, it must dissolve into secularism? By reacting in this manner, instead of fulfilling the responsibility it must assume in view of any religious definition of the technological phenomenon, Christianity, sadly enough, only tries to squirm out of its difficulty. And squirm it does. From numbness, of course, rather than dumbness. One may call it a lack of faith, or, what amounts to the same thing, a lack of an ecclesiology equal to the technological phenomenon.

Rather than aggravate the present crisis by playing the game of secularism, Christianity should analyze and comprehend technological religiosity—all the more so since it is quite likely that this religiosity continues to bear the marks of Christianity, if only because this religiosity belongs to a cultural environment permeated by Christianity.

We may indeed have abandoned a certain religious conception of the world but surely not for a non-religious one. Insofar as the present crisis is cultural, we are only exchanging one religious mentality for another. On the other hand, to the extent that this crisis is religious, we are on the threshold of a new era, on the crest of a new wave of civilization. We are moving from the universe of myth to the universe of technique.

The universe projected by the civilization of classical Christianity was a predominantly mythological universe. As we move into the predominantly technological universe of which our present civilization is but the forerunner, it might seem that religion is fading away. But in fact the religious imprint proper to each civilization is merely shifting from myth to technique, that is, changing denomination. Thus, in comparison with the sacred whose imprint is borne by the universe of myth, the mark of utopia characterizes religion in the universe of technique. We are passing over *from* a civilization whose symbol system is focused on the notion of salvation, that is, on man understood in terms of God or, if you will, on God as the condition for the realization of man, on man in the future tense; and we are passing over *to* a civilization whose symbol system, powered by the idea of the human as the happening of God, is focused on the notion of God understood in terms of man—focused, in other words, on the reign of God, on God in the present tense.

From this perspective, the present crisis is unprecedented.

Despite appearances, the twofold change through which this crisis is manifested implies much more than a reformation such as that of the sixteenth century. In that era the disruption no doubt shook the church to its foundations; but it challenged neither the value nor the validity of a civilization which still served as a context for the Christian faith and its policy of a destiny worthy of man.

Regardless of what the parties involved may have thought, the differences in mentality between the Reformation and the Middle Ages are in fact much less sharply defined than those between the New Testament and the Old. The religiosity upon which the self-understanding of Reformation man is based is just as mythological as that holding sway over medieval man. Thus, as a man of the Middle Ages, Luther was reduced to wrestling with the problem: "What must I do to be saved?" When he changed the formula and finally asked himself, "Who is this God who saves me?" the Middle Ages reached their end and Luther unleashed the Reformation. But he set off only a "reformation." Given the cultural affinities which persist even as one changes one's epoch and one's mentality, God himself was not yet seen as problematic. All told, the question posed by the sixteenth century did no more than ask whether one particular conception of God was better than another, whether God was really this rather than that. So much was this the case that when Catholics and Protestants confronted one another, it was

3

to do little more than relentlessly demonstrate either that the works of man were necessary *for the salvation* accomplished by God in Jesus Christ, or that they were not.

Today it is this very notion of salvation, the very idea of God, which is a problem. And for two reasons. On the one hand, there is no idea of God which does not directly depend on a particular cultural context.[1] No sooner is this context broken open than the reality of God, or at least Christianity's conception of it, is deprived of its footing. On the other hand, the idea of God is a problem precisely to the extent that it is the Christian conception of God which is put into question. At the same time contemporary Western man, hampered by the unavailability of any other conception of God to which he could have recourse, is less liberated than he imagines from a conception still Christian, if in name only. Hence man's experience of his own reality today, at least in the West, seems on balance to indicate a certain withholding of God.

B. The Church and the World

In previous days, reform sufficed to keep the believer from losing contact with the world, and faith, by virtue of its ecclesial structure, was intimately linked to the social structures of the

---

1. God is never God in general. Having promised a posterity to Abraham, God promised his descendants a land. But he becomes a God who reigns over the just as well as the unjust, as soon as the children of Israel are tempted to consider him a mere member of their household, a simple guarantee of their heritage. And so it is only normal that, by the rivers of Babylon, orphans of God and exiles, the children of Israel lament and mourn, wailing: "How shall we sing the Lord's song / In a foreign land?" (Ps. 137:4).

Subsequently, Christianity will simply revert to this idea that God himself is eclipsed if the civilization which legitimates his reality happens to disintegrate. This should not be surprising, since both Christianity and Judaism teach that God is closer to man than man is to himself. Yet in moving from Israel to the church, one difference nevertheless has appeared: instead of extolling descent from Abraham according to the flesh, Christianity proclaims that integration into the body of Christ is not a matter of descendence but of conversion. Knowing Christ according to the flesh is useless (2 Cor. 5:16; 1 Cor. 10:14—11:1). To know him is to know his benefits. It is as man, rather than as a descendant of Abraham, that man now has access to God. *Mutatis mutandis,* this signifies, of course, that the reality of God always necessarily calls for a cultural context, but with the difference that no longer is any cultural context better suited than another.

human reality itself. That is not to say the church is to be explained solely in terms of this manifestation of its undeniable solidarity with the world, a world which is ennobled by the fact that it thus serves as instrument for the advancement of man. It is nevertheless undeniable that, without the church, Christianity would have been only a "salvation" religion completely cut loose and disengaged from every concern for the world, fixed instead on the *other world*. Without the church, Christianity would already have succumbed to its wounds.

No doubt it is of the church that one usually thinks as soon as there is a question of denouncing the obsolescence of Christianity. As the praxis of faith, the church seems as outdated in the social as in the individual sphere. Even so, we must consider history honestly, without yielding either to triumphalism or to the prejudices of a systematic denigration whose power is all the more virulent in that for the most part it is armed with flagrantly anachronistic and otherwise specious argumentation. Though considerably dimmed, the light of history still allows us to see clearly. Without the church, the Gospel would have been from the very beginning merely an esoteric doctrine, and the Christian faith would now be no more than an occult doctrine with no future.

It is as a church that Christianity is ailing today. Yet, as in the apostolic age, it is also as a church that, humanly speaking, Christianity has a future.

Let us set aside the particular aspects with which history and its contingencies have subsequently clothed the notion of church: had Christianity been reduced simply to its theoretical dimension it would have been unable to take root; it would have survived neither Israel nor the *Pax Romana*. If it triumphed this was above all due to its idea of church, to its understanding of faith as encounter between God and man, that is, between the city of God and the terrestrial city. Without this cultural potential which the church represents in the name of the faith it attempts to incarnate, Christianity would have been no more than another mystery religion, one among many similar manifestations common in the Roman empire.

Christianity began with a cultural revolution, and unless it unleashes another, it will do no more than ratify its own condemnation. For neither the privatization of faith, nor the successive spurts of reform that only touch the theoretical dimension of faith, will enable Christianity to confront the cultural change engendered by the irresistible emergence of technological phenomena. In order to elicit, sustain, and affirm the quest for the human inherent in the technological phenomenon, Christianity must reformulate the very practice of its faith by reformulating itself in terms of its cultural capacity for accepting the technological phenomenon itself, and endowing it with radically new structures. But it has no other resource for this undertaking than an *ecclesial revolution.* Christianity in no way can proclaim salvation unless it can at the same time change the world.

For those who have forgotten, the point bears repeating: salvation, at least as the Gospel understands it, consists less in the imitation of Christ than in his coming into the world; it consists less in negating the world than in transfiguring it. In no way can Christianity be seen as one of those esoteric religions living off society and proliferating at the expense of the individual. One can at least say of Christianity that its understanding of salvation prohibits it from considering the world a forbidden zone it must evacuate. By the term salvation, Christianity understands the imminence or, better still, the immanence of God who rules in the world so that the world becomes the advent of the *novum,* the impossible possibility of the "fallen" world. Only insofar as it is new does the world escape chaos; it endures, as irresistible as hope when even hoping has been played out. God reigns, not because he could annihilate the world, but because he is its creator; he reigns, not because he could abandon the world, but because he is its destiny. As instrument of the God who reigns, the world is a new world, belonging to the *novum.* Inasmuch as it is also instrument of the *reign of God,* it belongs, fulfilled, to the *eschaton.* Advent of the *novum,* the world is event of the divine reality, of the *eschaton.* The fact must be underlined that even if it has all the traits of a salvation religion, Christianity prohibits any flight from the world. It refutes every form of escapism, whether through knowledge as initiation (gnosis) or through an initiation of the soul into its own principle (amnesis).

One must clearly affirm that what characterizes the logic of the Christian faith is in the last analysis less its notion of salvation than its notion of the kingdom of God, that is to say, its understanding of the world as instrument of the reign of God. What characterizes Christianity is less the soteriologism to which it has been assimilated than the utopianism which constitutes the axis of its Christological understanding of both God and man; it is, indeed, only in terms of a new world (because the world is world only if it can be changed) that God is its creator. Likewise, with respect to the new man, it is because man is something other than a "given" of nature that man is at once creature and condition of God.

In comparison with esoteric doctrines where salvation is understood as the soul's escape from the world, the Christian tradition does not hesitate to radicalize salvation. Indeed, it is impelled to do so as soon as it proclaims that there is no salvation outside the church, and that *consequently* there is no salvation without involvement in the world.

The essence of Christianity, a religion based on incarnation and hence on the time of the end, is an eschatological conception of the world, of man as well as of God. Thus Christianity is never at ease with an eschatology overtaken at one point by asceticism, at another by futurism, much less with an eschatology drifting in some nirvana which compels man to renounce humanity, or with an ideology which compels him to lose faith in man. Because it is essentially eschatological, Christianity is necessarily iconoclastic. To the extent that it is iconoclastic, Christianity is likewise eschatological. Accordingly, it challenges every negation of the utopianism proper to the human reality; and, moreover, it demands its radicalization, just as it demands the radicalization of salvation.

To repeat: even when Christianity appears as a salvation religion, its understanding of salvation is already essentially eschatological. And it is eschatological in such a way that it is manifested in an ecclesial conception of the kingdom of God, a conception in terms of which Christianity has distinguished itself from the very beginning, and thanks to which it proves itself capable of grasping and reinforcing the fundamental utopian dimension of the human reality.

C. God and the Utopian Reality of Man

This ecclesial approach to the utopian reality proper to man, corresponding to a similar approach to the reign of God, remains valid to this day. Over the centuries both have reflected various theological systems, now superannuated. The variations crystallize at two poles, one representing a metaphysical and the other a Christological orientation.

Both trends, however, evince a common problematic: whether God is thought of in terms of metaphysics or Christology, we are dealing with a conception of man or the world based on the necessity of the idea of God. From both points of view, one begins with the principle that God, hypothesis of all logic as well as preamble of every existential act, is the condition of everything that is. This principle is found as much in Saint Augustine or Saint Thomas as in Luther or Calvin. But while Saint Augustine sees no difference between the logic of thought and that of faith, Saint Thomas distinguishes these two orders, defining the logic of being as both presupposing the idea of God and fulfilling itself in the other world through the beatific vision of the "Wholly Other." Similarly, the idea of what God is *per se* plays a very important role in scholastic thought, while for the reformers the important thing is not what God is *per se* but what he does for man. Metaphysical at the outset, the logic of faith becomes Christological: it is in Christ—through Christ—that what God is for man is revealed.

It is true that, when man grasps his *ráison d'être* in this way, thinking finds a point of departure that does not offend its logic, while faith receives an assurance which does not dissolve it in "bad faith." But it remains no less true that, despite such different points of view, God is always conceived as the condition of man. We are still caught in the universe of myth, constrained and battered by its soteriological postulation of the relationship between God and man.

In the mythological universe of classical Christianity the soteriological tendency prevails over the eschatological. It does so to such an extent that faith itself runs the risk of being unable to survive the mythological folklore with which it is bound up.

Within the framework of a technological civilization whose principal characteristic is utopianism, the question is whether Christianity is capable of restoring the balance between these two tendencies and, moreover, of defining the structure of salvation by referring it to the reign of God. The question is whether the integrity of the human reality is bound up with a supernatural understanding either of the world or of transcendence. "The assumption which underlies the notion of a Christian existence growing out of and to be taken over from a Christian tradition was never genuinely present. It has now become quite impossible, and with it the notion itself."[2]

2. FROM THE DEIFICATION
OF MAN TO THE HUMANITY OF GOD

From the perspective of a civilization focused on salvation, God descends to the level of man, he stretches out his hand to man. As Saint Augustine puts it, God becomes man so that man may become divine. Conversely, from the perspective of a civilization focused on the reign of God, both man and the world are the event of the radical otherness of God. Attracted as much by one as by the other of these motifs, Christianity oscillates between the two. This is not to deny, however, that during its Constantinian mythological phase it leaned rather heavily toward the first, while now it leans—or should more clearly lean —toward the second, in the technological phase it still hesitates to enter.

The reason for this hesitation lies in the fact that Christianity is still encumbered by the heritage of a mythological mentality, even though it has been able to exchange the demiurgic concep-

---

2. Karl Barth, *Church Dogmatics* (T. & T. Clark, Edinburgh, 1936–1958), IV/3, II, sec. 71, 3, p. 524.

tion of God for one in which God is seen as the precondition
of all things, all beings.

A. The Death of God

After Copernicus, after Marx and Freud, after Nietzsche and
Einstein, contemporary man, whether he likes it or not, can no
longer account for his existence by arguing for the necessity of
the idea of God as an a priori. This difficulty might certainly
seem unreal, particularly to a believer still mentally cloistered
in the precincts of the supernatural. But whatever the weight of
his objection, it hardly counts for much, considering that such
a believer probably feels as if he belongs to two different worlds:
the world of his faith and the world which serves as the cultural
context for his daily life on the social, political, economic, and
ideological levels. A dichotomy of this kind would have been
unthinkable even in the midst of a civilization of salvation such
as Christendom once represented. It was even more so when,
in order better to adhere to faith, men went so far as to renounce the world completely: they renounced the world but
maintained their solidarity with it; they opted for a world that
was *other*. Against Athens, according to Tertullian's formula,
they opted for Jerusalem. In other words, they opted for the
transformation of the world.

It is one and the same language which permits us at the same
time to account for the reality (or vanity) of the world and within
it to attest the faith. One chooses faith, but in terms of an
understanding of the world which, far from competing with the
logic of this faith, actually immerses it in a greater intelligibility.
For the person who responds to the call of God is not the person
who avoids the world or withdraws from it, but the man or
woman who is emancipated, set free from it. Faith does not do
away with one's responsibility for the world any more than it
does away with the daily realities by which the man of flesh and
blood is molded. The whole Gospel brings home this one point:
it is concrete man, in a given historical situation which he assumes in its totality, that the Son of man comes to seek out and
save.

10

Today, when man thinks of the world or of his own reality, he thinks in terms that make traditional beliefs seem quite irrelevant. And, indeed, how is it possible for someone else's heart to beat within one's own breast? Nor is it thinkable that Adam, the man of clay into whose nostrils God must breathe the breath of life, should continue to represent man as a datum of nature, rather than as ultimately contesting it, precisely in keeping with the very notion of creation.

This is not to say that man today is less religious than he was in the past. But his religiosity is no longer shaped by the idea that God is the precondition of man. Other norms govern this religiosity. One could characterize it by saying, in general terms, that where it was once heteronomous now it is autonomous; where it was once theocentric now it is anthropocentric; where it was transcendental it is now immanentist.

From such a perspective, it is not the existence of God but his superfluousness which serves as hypothesis. The necessity of God is gnawed away and replaced by the autonomy of man; but it is of little consequence that this autonomy is but a pretense. An unbridled neo-polytheism now afflicts even the monotheism radicalized by the Christian tradition. All of this is what Kierkegaard sensed in the last century: a dead Christendom. He already realized the impossibility of being a Christian: the civilization which Christianity brought to life has become its tomb, at best its display case. And it is in every way logical that in an attempt to grasp the meaning of this failure in all its complexity, Nietzsche was led to proclaim the death of God. Nor is this blasphemy. Nietzsche's purpose was to denounce, at whatever cost, the pious lie which comforts us in our illusion that God can continue in his role as condition of man when, in fact, he has already been reduced to little more than an extra on the scene. If we watch the collapse and disintegration of Christendom through the critical eye of Kierkegaard, with Nietzsche we attend the collapse of theism; more precisely, Nietzsche points to the collapse of God as a postulate. Like Kierkegaard before him, Nietzsche announces the religious as well as cultural change of which the West today is still the object, if not the victim.

To be sure, when change is of such magnitude, consciousness of it can only emerge gradually. The erosion of divine transcendence, broached well before Nietzsche, thus is to be realized in successive stages, leading to an understanding of the world and of man which is not based on God as the precondition of man. It is also appropriate here to call attention to the fact that this erosion (or this leveling down and resultant rejection of God) is progressive and irreversible, manifesting itself differently in different periods: now in politics, now in ethics, now in science. It is first of all in the external world (of objects, institutions, and customs: the world of science) that theism is abandoned long before one even becomes aware of it. With the beheading of the "king by the grace of God," theism as the sanction for political and social organization is thrown into question by a kind of empiricism which at once questions man and throws him back upon himself. As Pascal emphasized, the same act can be seen as the act of a hero or the act of a murderer. And Laplace was on the verge of reporting a *fait accompli* when he responded to Napoleon's astonishment at hearing that God could be excluded from the scholar's system: "Sire, I have no need of that hypothesis." The man who aspires to self-knowledge no longer needs to venture forth beyond the sphere inscribed by the experience of his own reality; nor must he reach beyond the limitations of daily life and call upon a principle of explanation, a God beyond the world. This God, a hypothesis-god banished from the external world, will sooner or later be banished from the inner world, from human subjectivity itself. So inner man will also inevitably be emancipated from tutelage to theism.

Under these conditions, how can theology afford the luxury of referring to a God hypothesis?

Sooner or later theology will be forced to face the obvious; as Bonhoeffer remarks, it will one day be forced to admit that such a God is no more than a stopgap, a crutch—the opposite of the God of Abraham, Isaac, and Jacob, the opposite of the God of Jesus Christ. Otherwise, we would have to admit that the reality of God, to which the Bible witnesses, was dependent on a particular vision of the world.

This is in fact the question posed by Rudolf Bultmann in his

1941 essay on the New Testament and demythologization.[3] In stressing that the reality of God cannot depend on any particular vision of the world, Bultmann immediately inaugurates a revolution in theological method. In the wake of this revolution, in the very pursuit of his theological research and with a concern for the honesty of faith, he is—perhaps in spite of himself—once more the person who obliges us to adopt if not to assume the methodological atheism so characteristic of contemporary thought.[4]

But in forcing theology to abandon the intellectual artifice of the God hypothesis, the same cultural event which constitutes the death of God endows it with the possibility of facing anew the living God of the Bible, of discovering him in all his tangibility, in his contingency to the reality of the world, to the reality of man with all his greatness and weakness. The incarnation of the word links God's destiny to man's. But now it is the human, which, as a consequence of the collapse of theism, finally appears as what it really is in itself: the condition of God. No longer confusing God with theism as a method of universal explanation, theology only loses a world (that of Ptolemy) and a dialect (that of Canaan).

B. Beyond Theism and Atheism:
The Human as Condition of God

The crisis of civilization affecting us today is thus both religious and cultural; it can be truly grasped only when it is seen as a recurrence of this complex phenomenon which we call the death of God. Conversely, this implies that we are describing—or should be—an exclusively cultural phenomenon when we speak of the death of God. Unfortunately, this is not always the case. In fact, some writers thought that they could even further radicalize the meaning of the death of God by simply starting

---

3. Rudolf Bultmann, "New Testament and Mythology," in *Kerygma and Myth,* I, edited by H. W. Bartsch (S.P.C.K., London, 1953).
4. The reader would do well not to confuse methodological atheism with atheism *tout court.* The first refers to a working hypothesis which does not presuppose the existence of God, while the second postulates the latter's nonexistence.

with a new concept of salvation: man is no longer saved *by* God through the sacrifice of his son, but man must save himself *from* the God who himself died in Jesus Christ. Thus, these authors' formerly theistic presuppositions are simply replaced by a similar set of atheistic presuppositions. From our point of view, however, the death of God invalidates both sets of presuppositions in favor of a method (*not* a new soteriology) which postulates neither the existence nor the nonexistence of God. Thus, according to the degree of submission to the preconceptions of atheism, one can distinguish atheistic Christianity and kenotic atheism on the one side, and crypto-theistic kenotism on the other.[5]

As far as atheistic Christianity is concerned,[6] it seems that the death of God constitutes a sort of demarcation line between the Christian era with its essentially religious and theistic conception of the world and the nascent post-Christian era with its disillusioned secularist idea of a world in which God would only be so much excess baggage. From the transcendentalism of the past only that which can be retrieved in terms of total immanence deserves to be retrieved. And so the Gospel is reduced to the man Jesus and the exemplarity of his humanitarian message. But atheistic Christianity cannot shore up its defense ex-

---

5. It is not impossible—it is even probable—that words such as "kenotic" and "kenotism" or "crypto-theistic" grate against the sensibilities of the contemporary man without the moorings of the Christian tradition. As far as "kenosis" is concerned, it is a word of Greek origin which the Latin renders by a word which yields the English "exinanition." With this term classical theology attempts to indicate the self-abasement to which Christ voluntarily submits as he suffers the agony of the cross, as expressed in Phil. 2:5: "Let your bearing towards one another rise out of your life in Christ Jesus. For the divine nature was his from the first. Yet he did not think to snatch at equality with God, but made himself nothing [in Greek: *ekenosen*], assuming the nature of a slave. Bearing the human likeness, revealed in human shape, he humbled himself, and in obedience accepted even death—death on a cross." Whatever interpretation one gives this passage, it is clear that this text in no way stipulates that the movement of self-abasement, *kenosis*, results in some kind of vacant divinity (as atheistic Christianity would like to pretend). Kenotic atheism has even discovered this, and tries to correct the error by sallying forth in the other direction, conceiving of *kenosis* as the self-abasement of God preliminary to his rebirth through the concomitant apotheosis of man. Finally, by attributing to kenotism the quality of crypto-theism, I simply wish to emphasize the fact that it is neither clearly atheist nor clearly theist, and that, despite appearances, it does not situate itself beyond atheism, much less beyond theism and its traditional presuppositions.
6. Cf. William Hamilton, *The New Essence of Christianity* (Association Press, New York, 1966).

cept at the cost of a fatal negligence: if traditional theism (where God is conceived as the condition of man) collapses with the death of God, the same is true for atheism. Atheism—Christian style or otherwise—is no less overcome than theism, and the conflict which set them in opposition loses all its meaning. To be sure, in saying that one's image of God was part of a particular conception of the world, atheistic Christianity considers the death of God a cultural phenomenon. But it makes this the basis of a new soteriology by claiming that the very reality of God must be linked to a single conception of the world, and precisely that conception whose obsolescence forces us to stumble in a world henceforth deprived of the presence of God.

If atheistic Christianity makes for a secularized humanism, kenotic atheism[7] deplores the secularization of the world and makes for a religiosity inspired less by the faith of Israel than by ancient mythology and mystery cults. It is, in fact, the myth of the God who dies to be reborn which serves as model here. And to the extent that such a myth is based on the opposition between God and man, God must empty himself of his substance *(kenosis)* and die so that man can be. We are thus dealing with a sort of deicidal Oedipus, whom an intensely mystical speculation attempts to redeem through the death of God. The death of God thus ceases to be a cultural phenomenon and turns into a kind of divine suicide. Without entering into the details of this controversy—which is after all quite dated already —let us simply point out that for both Israel and Christianity there is never any idea of a basic opposition between God and man, but rather a convenant between creator and creature which determines everything else; there is no need for God to die so that man can be. Nor is it the case that God *is* only if man is nothing.

In principle, crypto-theistic kenotism[8] should essentially hark back to a doctrine declared heretical by the early church. According to this doctrine, God the Father himself undergoes the passion and death of his Son. On the cross, God annihilates

---

7. Cf. Thomas J. J. Altizer, *The Gospel of Christian Atheism* (Westminster Press, Philadelphia, 1966).
8. Cf. John A. T. Robinson, *Honest to God* (Westminster Press, Philadelphia, 1963); Jean Cardonnel, *Dieu est mort en Jésus-Christ* (Ducros, Bordeaux, 1967).

himself in order to let man come to his own and turn away from the false Gods he forges so as to reassume himself. Jesus Christ represents both the utter self-emptying to which God submits as well as the ultimate affirmation of man as freedom. Thus, if crypto-theistic kenotism does not entirely avoid the problem of God, it grants the death of God a status other than one belonging to cultural phenomenology. It attempts to honor contemporary atheism without at the same time selling out the Gospel. The result is a neo-pietism which, it seems, all too easily attributes to the world a role formerly played by the church, and to man the future of a destiny once dependent on God.

What characterizes these three Christian deviations, described very schematically above, is a tendency to reverse roles and put a minus sign where there was once a plus sign. Thus, instead of theism, it is atheism which serves as the mold for theological reflection; not the power, but the weakness of God now serves as a catalyst for the certainty of faith. Thanks to this permutation of roles, man henceforth imagines himself guaranteed the fullness of being, even to the extent that God empties and ultimately annihilates himself.

What possibilities remain, then, if we find traditional theology outdated, and yet must avoid the three pitfalls I have just indicated? Inasmuch as the task is both to free ourselves from the reassuring temptation of theism and yet not to succumb to that of atheist immanentism, it seems to me that a possible solution would consist of setting forth a theology which avoids falling back on the expedient of simply exchanging the roles of God and man. In order to do this, we must obviously also take into account the fact that the cultural phenomenon we call the death of God undermines not only theism but atheism as well, and above all the fact that the biblical understanding of God (contrary, no doubt, to what we are ordinarily led to believe) is itself clearly independent of theism. In effect, while theism, like every system, aims above all at explaining the world, for the Bible both the end of the world and its origin belong to the realm of eschatology: it is not necessary for the world to have a meaning in itself in order for it to proclaim the glory of God. God is not the precondition of all that is. But all that is is God's condition.

By explicitly stating that man is the condition of God, I avoid a simple reversal of roles. I avoid it because, from this perspective, that which all human reality attests is neither the presence of God (as in the days of absolute theism) nor his absence (as in the case of atheism or kenotism), but the otherness of God. God and man are thus not confused, nor are they arbitrarily distinguished from one another under the cover of a preliminary postulation of the existence of God. Is the New Testament saying anything different when it affirms that man has no access to God other than through this Jesus who is the human condition of the Christ, the condition of the reality of God? To be sure, such an approach to the problem of faith necessitates not so much a reversal of roles as a toppling of idols; it notably requires us to smash the idol that God becomes once we make either the world or man dependent upon him, as upon a universal principle of explanation. To be here, God needs no other support than man, and Christ is the condition of the man who assumes the condition of God.

3. THE TRANSCENDENCE OF GOD AND TECHNOLOGICAL UTOPIANISM

A. Obsolescence or Ecclesial Revolution?

In the context of an increasingly provocative technological civilization, one particular conception of Christianity is already obsolete. But it is not technique as such which condemns Christianity to total and irreversible obsolescence. The decadence of Christianity can be imputed neither to the erosion of the transcendence of God nor to its leveling down in favor of a compensatory immanentism which remains full of illusion; nor can we thereby wholly account for the reduction of theology to a subset of anthropology, or the reduction of God to man. Similarly, if Christianity is becoming totally obsolete, this cannot be blamed on the extinction of the universe of myth beneath the spectacular as well as irresistible thrust of technological phenomena as cultural innovators. We will attribute this collapse to the blindness of a Christianity which refused to adapt to technique and to new forms of religiosity at once consonant with technological civilization and distinguishing it from so-called Christian civilization as well as every other form of mythological civilization.

It is, perhaps, in relation to the notion of divine transcendence that this new religiosity diverges from traditional mythological religiosity. For the latter, the human reality is inevitably caught in the tension between the polarities of "here below" and "beyond," of past and future. And, over against the supernatural, nature appears as a counter-nature, whereas history becomes the *contretemps* of a sacred time always envisioned as the sacred time of the origins.

Undoubtedly, the tripartite conception of the universe in which the earth is trapped between heaven above and hell below rather handily removed the obstacles to the formulation of divine transcendence. And, in like manner, it was quite simple to define this transcendence in terms of the exteriority of God to the world, especially since man, given his tendency to understand himself as a more or less immutable datum, was seen as belonging either to the order of nature or to the order of history.

But obviously it is not so much this divine exteriority itself which is creating a problem today, but the fact that it has been reduced to a mere belief. Such a belief is no less inappropriate for us than is the science of Ptolemy, even if both can still be understood. It is not so much the metaphysical aspect of this conception of transcendence which disturbs us, as its anchorage in the supernatural. What is similarly disturbing is the ideological tendency lurking behind a historicizing consciousness which reflects the same conception of transcendence, and for which "the end of the world" is merely the counterpart of "the other world."

Clearly, in the technological vision of the human, such conceptions of divine transcendence flagrantly offend the integrity of man if only because they are supernatural or apocalyptic. They no longer challenge man because they no longer have the strength or the power to do so. Very simply, they have lost their credibility.

I am not saying that we should forgo these notions or ideas about transcendence merely because they are not compatible with the data of contemporary science. What we must forgo is the mentality in which they are steeped: a mentality corresponding to the constraints of a mythological religiosity where such conceptions govern an ecclesial organization of faith, and whose sole effect is to paralyze the latter precisely at a time when it must confront the technological phenomenon, the religiosity of which it must acknowledge and explore. Nor am I saying that the Christian faith must accommodate itself or bend to the solicitations of the religiosity peculiar to technological civilization. I am simply saying that at the heart of the problem of technique, we find ourselves confronted with a religious problem.

But this is a problem of such magnitude that Christianity will not be able to come to grips with it without a cultural revolution, that is, an ecclesial revolution. The victory which faith represents is surely a victory over the world. But to accomplish this victory, faith must address itself to the world; it must start by listening to the world. On the basis of the validity of its response to the challenge being posed by the world, on the basis of the legitimacy it draws from the question of the world, faith manifests itself as other than belief, custom, or knowledge.

Furthermore, it will first of all be necessary for church structures to be cast in the mold of technological civilization. For it is through the church that the transcendence of God is engaged: a transcendence no longer conceived of from a speculative point of view, but from a liturgical (i.e., political, ethical, sociocultural) point of view. Through the church the transcendence of God is no longer a state or an attribute by which God is distinguished from man; it is an undertaking in which, as the word becomes flesh, God collaborates with man and man with God. God is transcendent precisely to the extent that his transcendence does not entail his exile from the world. If God reigns, it is neither over another world nor over (or beginning with) the end of the world, but over a world that is *other*.

B. Transcendence: From the Myth of Man to the Human as a Technique

It could be argued that Christianity itself has given birth to technology. But there is no need to go that far. It is enough to call attention to the fact that without Christianity technology would not be what it is today. Reciprocally, Christianity is linked to technology to such an extent that without technology Christianity would be little more than a vestige.

In so emphasizing the intimacy of the relationship between Christianity and technology, I am only trying to point out one thing: how mistaken we would be if we continued to conceive of God's transcendence in terms of a model drawn from a soteriological view of man rather than an eschatological vision of the human reality and its utopianism—that is, in terms of myth rather than technology. Accordingly, we would do well, first of all, to recall what is at stake when we move from myth to technology as a framework for religious understanding.

Considering this phenomenon from a historical point of view, we will try to account for it by briefly examining (1) the double process of Christianity's acculturation and secularization, (2) the result of this process: the decline of myth as a framework of religious understanding and its collapse with the death of God, and (3) the emergence of technology as a framework of religious understanding or, more precisely, the emergence of a new *technique* of the human which is a technique centered neither on a sacral nor on an apocalyptic but on a utopian conception of transcendence.

(1) The Acculturation of Christianity and Its Secularization
By "acculturation" I mean to indicate the process which has led Christianity to become confused with the civilization it has itself secreted and thereby to remain trapped within it. This is the risk Christianity cannot wholly avoid taking as long as it refuses to advocate religious esotericism or escape from the world. Since its attitude toward the world is more positive than negative, Christianity affirms the world far more than it seeks to deny it. Following the Old Testament, it does not take the world as

something divine or consider nature as personifying the reality of God. Iconoclastic to the end, it affirms that God the creator, the God who reigns, is the only God who is holy. In consequence, Christian iconoclasm is translated, at least in appearance, into a desacralization of nature: the world is not given once and for all, it is a possibility which God grants to man and grants him continually. Apart from the fact that man has a right to this world, he is also responsible for it; so much so that he would be renouncing his right if he abdicated his responsibility. Furthermore, he can only exercise the latter by claiming the world as a sign of the unique holiness of God.

I am not convinced of the appropriateness of the term desacralization in defining an approach which not only attempts to be but is much more iconoclastic than desacralizing; and I am even less convinced when, in addition, what such an approach seeks to denounce is the profanation of the world as well as idolatry, locking God up in the images man makes of him. In the biblical view, the world in itself is neither sacred nor profane: it is an instrument of the holiness of God.

This distinction is important; from it flows a conception of nature which results in neither its sacralization nor its profanation but, rather, in biblical language, in its sanctification—that is to say, its transformation, its being taken in charge as much *by* man as *for* man. Nor is such an approach without importance: it rescues nature from the necessity of personifying any divinity. In divinizing nature man certainly has no other purpose than to humanize it better. The question, however, is whether nature can then truly serve as a paradigm of the human. Fully aware of the delicacy of this question, the biblical approach tackles it, but not without reversing the terms: it is the human which must serve as a paradigm of nature. Not that man thus escapes nature; but he is no longer its victim or its afterthought. After all, doesn't the man who divinizes nature feel out of place there? And, lacking any sense of solidarity with nature, does he then have any alternative but to profane it?

In biblical thought this conception of man is replaced by another which places man in solidarity with nature but does not make him its vassal, its burden.

In a parallel way, the cycle of seasons where nature (unless it

falls into abeyance) must, so to speak, renew itself and rediscover its sources in the sacred time of the origins, gives way to
another cycle: the sacramental cycle of the liturgy, where this
same nature is now the promise of a new nature, and where, as
Feuerbach so well perceived, man finally becomes conscious of
nature as nature.

It does not follow, however, that the emergence of such a
consciousness is free from all ambiguity. As a credence which
is, alas, irretrievable, the sacred emigrates. From nature it emigrates to the supernatural: even so, this is not illogical since the
Most High is also the Most Holy. Or, already seeking to repudiate myth, it takes refuge in history; this too is logical since man
henceforth conceives of himself as responsible for the world,
and this responsibility cannot be exercised except where the
word becomes flesh, where the world is conceived of in terms
of man as a becoming, as futurable.

As for the transcendence of God, it passes from a symbol
system governed by the notion of epiphany (the space where the
sacred time of the origins suspends all history) to a symbol
system governed by the notion of apocalypse (the end of time,
where for want of being able to change the world or hold it at
bay, the only thing left is to change worlds). In fact, nothing
happens but this: God reigns but he reigns only over a world
which eludes him as well as us. And faith becomes rigid, freezes.
No longer centered on the utopianism of the kingdom of God,
faith is immobilized in a conception of salvation on which the
church holds the monopoly: no salvation outside the church.
Salvation understood in such a way that in spite of the eschatological character of faith, what follows as a consequence is,
increasingly, a gaping dichotomy between the church and the
world. Under the cover of desacralization, what takes place is a
simple transference of the sacred, as a result of which the world
finds itself profaned. It will be colonized by the church.

Yet, the church is simultaneously in the process of secularizing itself. God withdraws from the world, and we begin to sense
his superfluity the moment we compare the world to a clock. As
Pascal says in reference to Descartes, the scaffolding upholding
these two worlds, both natural and supernatural, can collapse
with a flick of the finger. What in fact collapses is an all too

peaceful system of thought which no longer manages to conceive of transcendence without banishing God from the real world, a banishment whose true cause must be attributed to the atrophy of the idea of God. By simply reducing God to a principle explaining man and the world, we yield to the temptation to exalt the explanation at God's expense, the signifier at the expense of the signified. In the final analysis we submit the very idea of God to the obligation which reason is itself led to honor by conforming its own norms to those of science.

By conceiving of God as the unique principle of total explanation, we risk conceiving of *nothing but* technique.

(2)The Decadence of Myth as Framework
of Religious Understanding
From myth to technique the passage is realized through the death of God. Not that technique can only mediate an exclusively atheistic conception of God and the world. Were it so, technique would cease to be scientific.

In itself incapable of postulating the existence of God, technique cannot postulate his nonexistence any better. Contrary to myth, which tends to perceive man above all in terms of salvation, technique, neutral in this respect, has a propensity for utopia. It eludes, accordingly, every conception of human reality according to which man would test the presence or absence of God, his nearness or distance, his transcendence beyond the world or his immanence. Besides being favored by the outcome of a double process in which the acculturation of Christianity and its secularization culminate in the death of God, technique brings an end to the mythological conception of transcendence, whether in its sacral or its apocalyptic version.

But technique does not exclude God. It only eliminates the presuppositions by which God becomes the object of human experience, now by his presence, now by his absence. It hardly excludes—far from it—the possibility of articulating the transcendence of God as God's radical otherness, which man attests precisely to the extent that he experiences his own integrity. Technique thus marks the birth of a new form of religiosity, at once heir to and negation of the Christian tradition, at once its fulfillment and its denial.

Nor is it an unimportant characteristic of technique that it is tributary to the iconoclasm through which faith is manifested, and thanks to which, if we admit that man has emancipated himself from nature, we must also admit that nature has been no less emancipated from man. Participating in one and the same creation, each receives its due: man, what is proper to nature, and nature, what is proper to man—and neither is diminished. To note the importance of this transformation is to note the emergence of a new religiosity, the very one that explains today's reversal of the roles of science and technology; science is henceforth an element of technology, and the latter encompasses the former.

Moreover, colliding with science throughout the modern era, Christianity is left maimed. By contrast, technology in the meantime transcends science and prevents man from simply being reduced to a set of scientific givens. Scarcely negligible, this is the result of the cultural change wrought by the birth of a new form of religiosity. Others, like Jacques Ellul, have already called attention to it: with technique, we are no longer talking about tools or machines or even automation. We are dealing with a methodology, a vision of man and the world. Attuned to technology, a new religiosity is opening up new ways of invoking God, as did previous religiosities modeled on nature as God's footstep, or on history as the act of God.

(3) The Emergence of Technology as
Religious Framework of Understanding
In biblical thought, faith—the reality of man who is not man unless he is new man—is centered on both iconoclasm and eschatology. Iconoclastic, it belies all idolatry, and yet does not turn itself into an instrument of the profanation of the world. Eschatological, it engages the reign of God when it is engaged in the world, but it must be engaged in the world since it can but engage the reign of God; and yet it does not offer itself, surreptitiously, as an instrument for the resacralization of the world. Instrument neither of profanation nor of sacralization, faith is above all a crucible of the human—of everything human, whatever its vector, or whatever the matrix of the religiosity

challenging the human. Depending on the epoch, one matrix or another—now nature, now history—enjoys preponderance, if not exclusiveness, and determines the framework of religious understanding. (Let us note in passing that these religious matrices correspond to as many mythological conceptions of the world. As Clement of Alexandria noted, mythical or not there is no reason for not making use of these matrices, especially if they help to clarify the proclamation of faith.) Whatever the circumstances, and Karl Barth's views on the subject notwithstanding, faith consists less in the abolition of religion than in the transfiguration of the world.

From the point of view of primitive man, nature is anonymous: he personifies it. As insatiable as it is inexhaustible, nature remains hostile or at least indifferent to man. The more he belongs to it, the more he is bound to feel superfluous. When nature governs man, indeed, the gods themselves are never superfluous. At least not so long as they do not die.

By contrast, in biblical thought nature is now linked to the destiny of man, and not to the metamorphoses of the gods. Unlike Atlas, who has to conquer the world and push back its borders simply so that he can support it, man, created in the image of God, does not have to endure the world but determine its worth. In the hands of man, nature can become natural. Man is no longer at the mercy of nature; he thanks God for it.

The idea of the world as creation in no way results in a divorce between man and nature, nor does it subjugate nature to man. But since it results in a conception of man that renders him responsible for nature, then it is through man that nature becomes conscious of itself as nature and is transformed into a *project.* To the extent that the identity of God, his name, is no longer dissolved in the anonymity of nature, the world acquires a utopian dimension—it is worth a paradise. But this paradise is so strictly contingent on man's fidelity to his own vocation that it is paradise only if man, in the wake of Adam, does not abdicate his own responsibility, his humanity. As soon as Adam yields to the serpent's prompting he confuses paradise with nature and loses both. There is no paradise without nature. Much less, however, is there nature without paradise. To attain

25

paradise, it is not enough to break with nature. Nor must nature be abandoned to corruption: given over to nature, paradise is lost.

Paradise does not consist in man's setting himself up like a god in nature but in making of nature a world where creation can burst forth. "O Lord, our Lord, how great is your name throughout all the earth" (Ps. 8:1).

Thus when creation breaks forth in the world, it is not in terms of nature, much less in terms of a nature taking the place of a lost paradise, that the "nature" of man is to be understood. Rather, it is in terms of the promised land, the New Jerusalem. It is in terms of the reign of God that the human is the prolepsis of man.

The biblical notion of creation thus works as long as transcendence participates not merely in a sacred but in a utopian vision of the human reality. The same applies to the biblical view of incarnation. Here, too, occurs the development of a utopian conception of transcendence which runs counter to the sacral notion of time.

For the latter, history in fact represents only a profaning movement away from the sacred time of the origins; man can only hope to become what he is through a return to the sources. But then history is only a narrative, a drama which ends as soon as man enters the scene.

In contrast, the incarnation means that the transcendence of God need not be reabsorbed into the space of a sacred time of the origins at the threshold of history. It means that this transcendence is an integral part of the becoming of man. In the same way that creation valorizes a utopian conception of nature, the incarnation emphasizes a utopian conception of history, and in particular of the very historicity of the human condition. Man need no longer return to the sources in order to finally become that which he is; he can henceforth become that which he is not, namely, here and now the condition of divine transcendence. In Christ, man becomes that which he is not: he becomes a new creature for whom everything becomes new, that is to say, an event of the God who reigns. Henceforth, history is no longer narrative or loss of meaning, but a scenario of destiny; the gods who die and are reborn make way for the God who is, who was, and is to come, for the *eschaton*.

C. From Technological Utopianism to the Reign of God

But what relationship can all this have to the religiosity which has supposedly emerged from the cultural mutation brought about by the rise of technology? Such a question is not as disconcerting as it might at first seem. The answer, in any case, is rather simple.

Let us begin by drawing attention to the fact that what is important in the biblical perspective of creation and redemption, as well as of the pleroma which is their complement (as we shall see later), is a double preoccupation. It is concerned less with affirming nature or history than with the transcendence of God. And it is likewise concerned less with affirming nature or history than with the human: the word takes on man's form in the same way that God creates man according to his image. Or, more precisely, it is due to God's transcendence that nature acquires a significance, and history a meaning. And it is due to the human, moreover, that this transcendence does not lose itself in nature or dissolve itself in history. This means that since God is no longer confused with nature or bound to history, at the same time man is removed from determinism, from the realm of necessity characterizing history and nature.

Under these conditions it does not seem possible to envisage the relationship of Christianity to the emergence of technology, except by starting with such givens. More precisely, we must try to understand Christianity's aptitude for technology and do so only by relating it to the affirmation which safeguards the transcendence of God and establishes the human as the prolepsis of man, and not by referring it to the curse whose object Adam becomes (he must earn his bread by the sweat of his brow) in supposedly mastering and dominating a nature from which he is alienated. Or, to put it in theological language, we must not attempt to analyze technology by referring back to the Fall; this would falsify our understanding of the one as well as the other. On the contrary, we must seek the charter of technology in the original goodness of creation itself. Moreover, if we take into account the fact that what distinguishes technology is its way of annulling both nature as necessity and history as determinism, then we can only stress all the more the bond uniting technological utopianism to the utopianism manifested by the biblical understanding, whether of divine transcendence or of the human reality.

From the points of view of both technology and the Christian tradition, man cannot make his proper place unless there is a place for man which is neither residue of nature nor afterglow of history. Man remains to be realized. Thus, both technological and Christian utopianism inaugurate an ethic of the coming man, an ethic of the "future life"; the life which God alone can reserve for man, for him "who shall live even though he be dead."

Thus, if only provisionally, we can conclude the threefold analysis we have sketched with a view to grasp the nature of the identity crisis currently being experienced by Christianity, to appreciate its scope, and to isolate what is at stake. Is Christianity still capable of forging a new identity for itself? If so, under what conditions?

Whether we like it or not, all of us, inasmuch as we are at the dawn of the year 2000, have opted for a technological civilization. From a human point of view, there is only one way out, a way revealed in the logic of the examination we have just concluded. This way out is pointed up by Christianity's need to rethink its fidelity to divine transcendence by reassessing man's place in the world in terms of the reign of God as a presupposition of salvation, rather than of salvation as a presupposition of the reign of God; in terms of eschatology rather than soteriology; in terms of the utopianism of transcendence rather than a transcendence merely sacral or apocalyptic.

We will certainly have to shore up such propositions. Yet I believe that if Christianity becomes exclusively dependent upon a mythological understanding of salvation, it will risk yielding to the temptation of esotericism, precisely because, in one sense, technology similarly favors esotericism; when threatened, man takes refuge where he can. To be sure, evasion by means of the soul is a form of utopianism, but one which has the inconvenience of being compatible only with the sacral or apocalyptic understanding of transcendence. It is compatible only with an ascetic ideal of life. The asceticism of classical utopianism is explained less by a desire to renounce the world than by the conditions of scarcity to which common life submits. For poverty, especially when involuntary, deserves only to be eradicated, and to eradicate it one must be rich (in the goods of the spirit, but in material goods as well). Technological utopianism starts with a complete transvaluation of all our values. In technological terms, every problem is by definition soluble. But when it is possible to eradicate the cause of an evil the way one solves a problem, there is no virtue in opposing evil. Much less is there one that could give rise to any ideal of life, let alone to any eschatological iconoclasm of the alienating power of which every society is a victim.

Formerly, nature was the wholesale proliferation of symbols, so much so that the problem was to avoid engulfing or annexing the transcendence of God through it; thus the church, with good reason, conceived of the salvation proferred by Christ as an ascetic expectation of the reign of God. Soon, however, salvation and reign of God no longer coincide: they are separated and, given the current situation, they become imcompatible—or nearly so. Only at the end of time will God truly reign, in another world.

We have tried to show that a church for our time can no longer be satisfied with an ascetic interpretation of the reign of God. As Jesus stressed, it is not enough to have Abraham as father, for God can raise up descendants of Abraham even from stones (Matt. 3:9; Luke 3:8). We must not forget that God is never transcendent, is never the radically other, except where his word is incarnated and fulfilled in raising up new scriptures.

Where symbols become silent because they have become no more than *givens* of nature or history instead of representing their *charisms,* this is where the word becomes flesh. And where the word becomes flesh is where the church appears: community of the *eschaton* as well as body of Christ, gift as well as natural or historical given, both salvation and kingdom, advent of God and reign of God.

What does the church signify, if not the fact that outside the *reign* of God there is no salvation? Thus understood, the church would only be more capable of fulfilling its iconoclastic vocation against the very sacralization of the radical otherness of God and the no less alienating profanation of man and the world.

At one time the sole instrument of salvation, the church responded to the needs of a society for which God symbolized immutability. Today there is no society apart from its changes, no world apart from its transfigurations. And technological civilization is understood as an opportunity for, if not as a means of, changing the world—and man. How could the dwelling place of God, his reign and his transcendence, be otherwise if they must be established among men? Moreover, is not the incarnation of the word—where God no more engulfs man than he allows himself to be engulfed—the anticipation of a utopian understanding of transcendence and, simultaneously, of man come to terms with the phenomenenon of technology, with technique?

"If the salt loses its savor, with what will it be seasoned?" If, then, the technological world has not yet developed its gifts, it lacks more than a simple cultural revolution. If it still lacks savor, what it needs is an *ecclesial* revolution.

II

Ideology, Utopia, Eschatology

To live in the present: this, ultimately, is the heart of the matter, whether one copes with ideology and utopia or with eschatology.[1] To live in the present—as it were, for the first time. No eschatology can provide the recipe for this, unless it imitates utopia or parodies ideology, and thereby denies either the iconoclastic vision of the former or the charismatic ambition of the latter. Faith, a choice one must make without being forced, is a matter of decision and invention, not of inventory.

No wonder, then, that ideology and utopia are the two temptations of eschatology. But they are its safeguards, too. They resemble it as much as (for different reasons) they differ from it.

Precision about the specific meaning of each term is therefore quite important. We must, however, bear in mind that in defining one of them, we may also happen to define the other two. The reason is that all three of them beam a language whose words say the same thing even if they sound different and sound different even if they mean the same thing.

Then why bother with all of this, especially if it is only a matter of words?

Because words are merely words only if, precisely, one "hears" them and, through them, "sees" somewhat more clearly.

---

1. If I should claim that I know what is meant by ideology I would be lying. I would be lying even more if I should pretend to know nothing about it. Nor can utopia more easily be defined, except by dreaming that which it is not. It is by dreaming that utopia rings true. But it lies as soon as it allows itself to be caught dreaming.

It is, finally, by sounding true that eschatology finds a dream, just as it is by adhering closely to the real that one can *imagine* its true reality, quite a different thing from the image of man merely outliving the past.

Man comes at the price of the human. The futurable par excellence, the human as the reality of man, the eschatic reality of the new man—these are ultimately what ideology and utopia, as well as eschatology, all deal with.

1. IDEOLOGY

As a critique of uncritically endorsed ideas, ideology aims at a single goal—bringing man back within the only realm which knowledge can assign him, even if death, while demythologized, does not quite succeed in banishing anxiety. Doubtless itself a demythologizing factor, ideology certainly owes its initial success to the fact that it arises among ruins; it is raised from the ruins of thought or of belief once these become entangled in the webs of systems justifying their respective alibis[2] by the deficiencies of a world[3] where the only thing real, from failure to failure, amounts to holding up underdeveloped and over-exploited man on the threshold of the human. Since Feuerbach, ideology starts off by sinking God in man and by replacing theology with anthropology.

Whatever the truth, nothing is more difficult than trying to anchor the authority needed to affirm that truth in something besides faith. Only when it is too late do we realize this: man is what he eats, according to the devastating formula of Feuerbach. Yet we must still know who this man is. The atheist is never more than the accomplice of a God that fails. That is why, without prejudging the final import of the Marxist contribution to the status of ideology, one could argue that atheism by itself would not know how to warrant the autonomy which ideology lacks but claims for itself in criticizing adverse positions. Without the complicity of the past, it would have no future. But, since this past is dead and gone, the values ideology defines are, in any case, those of a bankrupt morality. Or, as Jacques Monod

---

2. For example, the futuristic notions of life after death, or of another world.
3. The deficiencies which these alibis inflict on the world by surrendering it to the status quo.

correctly points out, the failure of value systems brings with it the failure of the corresponding ideology.[4]

If ideology is evidence of a crisis, it is no less its symptom.

Not unlike scholasticism on the eve of the Renaissance, is it not at the decline of civilization that ideology appears? Quite plausible at that point, ideology must still look so subsequently, despite all the paraphrases to which it appeals as it attempts to survive in the very culture which gave it birth, and whose presuppositions it denounces while at the same time playing them in its favor. Denouncing presuppositions is one thing. Quite another is knowing what ethic these same presuppositions, transposed only to a new register, will authorize. The question is whether such a transfer will suffice to confer on these presuppositions the absolution they need, or whether it only brings them the self-satisfaction of being dissolved in a system. An ethic which would claim to be in no need of forgiveness would, in fact, be an absolutist and totalitarian ethic, a theodicy where man, misunderstanding his humanity, becomes a rival of God, the Babel rather than the Pentecost of man grappling with the spirit.

Ideology is what breeds and thrives on great shifts of civilization, shifts that choke up ethics. At first exuberant, it soon waxes dull from the weight of its own sclerosis. But ideology does not, for all that, give birth to ethics, except in terms of a stillborn ethic reduced to the ideology of an ethics. A self-styled dissenter, ideology is too dependent on the ethic it challenges not to become totalitarian itself.

One must point out, however, that regardless of how totalitarian it may be, all ideology is in reality a kind of makeshift utopia, just as, conversely, all utopia shifts into some ideology. Not that by thus determining the relations between ideology

4. Indeed, if religion could in the past usurp the role of science, ideology, as Jacques Monod points out, can similarly turn science into derision (Jacques Monod, *Chance and Necessity: An Essay in the Natural Philosophy of Modern Biology* [Knopf, New York, 1971]). To support Monod's thesis, one could cite two relatively recent cases. On the one hand, comes to mind the infamous Scopes trial of 1926, involving advocates of Darwin's theory as a subject matter for teaching science; on the other hand, there is the Lysenko affair which spawned the chronicles of the Stalin era around 1950. But we can only miss the question that confronts us here if, like Monod, we content ourselves with concluding that there is no ideology, just as there is no religion, without presuppositions.

and utopia, we must unavoidably confuse one with the other. Quite the contrary. Accordingly, our approach will consist, to begin with, in a clarification of the reasons ideology and utopia overlap, at least up to a certain point. In a second step, we will deal with utopia and its radicalization through eschatology. Taking the third step, we will broach the problem of language as advent, precisely of the very object of eschatology: namely, of the *eschaton*. We will thus be led to consider our problem from the angle of the denominator which utopia and ideology have in common, as well as with eschatology. Finally, we will conclude with a few remarks on hermeneutics and its quarrel with ideology.

2. IDEOLOGY AND UTOPIA

Agreeing with Karl Mannheim, we may see in the Anabaptist movement of the sixteenth century the harbinger of an unprecedented conception of ideology, if not simply the very birth of ideology itself. We must emphasize, however, that ideology and utopia, like two extremes, call upon and motivate one another while at the same time they diverge from one another just as quickly.[5] The key to their convergence is also that of their divergence. It consists in one and the same unique event, man's advent to a language by which he can possibly adhere to the world—not through mimetism or resignation, or even, as it were, because he needs to appease some promiscuous desire for the things of nature or for the order of history, but very simply by reason of the integral utopianism which grounds man by committing his own reality to the shape of a world whose "farside," the *eschaton*, is its only reality. Moreover, man's advent to language is such an event that it can no longer be understood as the occasion for some return to nature, any more than it can belong to history, since it appeals to ethics. But it appeals to an

5. Cf. Karl Mannheim, *Ideology and Utopia* (Harcourt Brace Jovanovich, New York, 1955).

ethics which can be accounted for only to the extent that it can account for the fulfillment of the human condition.

Realizing himself through speech alone, man fulfills his condition by taking off from nature as well as from history. This implies an ethics whose main characteristic thus consists in joining its inherent iconoclasm together with language, the eschatological locus of man's reality. Enrico Castelli is therefore correct: "It is not the event which proceeds from ideology; it is ideology which proceeds from the event."[6] Should we, then, give ideology a decidedly positive aspect, we could not in fact justify doing so if (perhaps unconsciously) we did not likewise justify that very thing with which we thought of contrasting ideology, whether it was knowledge, or belief, or customs (praxis).

Nor is it in relation to the degree of knowledge or the depth of belief, or even in relation to the breadth of praxis, that, whether by differentiating or identifying them, one recognizes ideology. Trying to reduce ideology to a system of assonances or dissonances would result, moreover, in corroborating what already constitutes one of its salient characteristics.

But it is in terms of event that we can hope to isolate it fully. In terms of event: that is, precisely in terms of that which eludes all praxis yet continues to provide it with a basis, of that which does not allow itself to be objectified by any knowledge, whose objectivity it yet guarantees. "I find it to be a law," says Saint Paul, "that when I want to do right, evil lies close at hand. For I delight in the law of God, in my inmost self, but I see in my members another law at war with the law of my mind and making me captive to the law of sin which dwells in my members" (Rom. 7:21–23). The ultimate deadline of freedom, praxis can just as easily divert such a freedom from its destiny, while belief, open though it is to every sacrifice, can just as easily prevent man from offering the only sacrifice that counts, that of a pure heart. As for knowledge, everyone knows what impotence weighs it down. In the last analysis, it stands resourceless before the contradictory demands of the two laws in the face of which, like Saint Paul, man knows and does not know himself, until he

---

6. Enrico Castelli, *Idéologie et démythisation* (Aubier, Paris, 1973).

is forced to cry out: "Who will deliver me from this body of death?" What event? The advent of Christ to man, says the apostle—or of man to the word, one could add, since only the event is capable of escaping the contradiction. Only his advent to the word allows man to preserve his authenticy in spite of all the constraints to which he bows, like a reed bending to the wind yet not breaking.

In contrast to practices, just as opposed to beliefs or knowledge, the advent of man to the word—or, very simply, to the event—cannot be usurped; it cannot be stockpiled. We can only inherit it. But, then, whoever, is merely its heir is by that fact its usurper, whether through what he knows, or through what he believes, or through what he practices. No event lords it over man. And yet it is sovereign. At the mercy of every praxis, of every belief, and of every system of knowledge, all preying on it even as they make vows of obedience to it, the event preserves its sovereignty like the alien who only discovers his identity in a foreign country. It is unique, and yet it depends so much upon the conjunction of circumstances that, personified, it would depend on the conjunction of the "other."

The event avoids being caught between the devil and the deep blue sea in dichotomies like belief and knowledge, theory and praxis. When it occurs, it always does so not from within them but from *elsewhere*, and we should only lose it entirely if we tried to place it between an *already* and a *not yet*. It is caught neither in the traps of the past nor in the snares of the future: it is what surprises, the *novum*. That is to say, it is that which can only take place. Having thus no place of its own, it can make room for utopia. It takes place only where all things find their proper place: language, where all knowledge is put together, all belief put to the test, all praxis put to the proof.

Coping with the event, ideology turns it into a commonplace. And yet (unlike some theology bogged down in its own logic, as if faith were simply a matter of self-management) ideology cannot be charged with misplacing it. Ideology is to utopia as language is to word, fault to forgiveness, sin to grace, sinful man to justified man. But since it is before God alone that justified man can acknowledge himself as sinner, and since, moreover, man speaks only by way of hoping for some forgiveness, ideology is not to be condemned either. It can only be forgiven. Just as all religion begins by desacralizing what it dissents from, so does all ideology begin by demythologizing what it stems from. Ideology will deny this, but it cannot, in the final analysis, come into its own except as a quest for forgiveness. In saying all that must be said it does not say what can be said, and disavows its own pretension. It disavows even the imagination which leads it to pretend it has *nothing more* to forgive itself or, rather, to be forgiven.

But what is forgiveness if not the breach through which grace takes away sin, through which language becomes speech, through which the world becomes event, preventing man from falling back either into nature, which has no sense of guilt, or into history, which has no reason for forgiveness? At the very heart of the dialectic of guilt and forgiveness, of sin and grace, the event takes place: it is incarnation rather than some return to the sources, especially if such a return must always presuppose *another world,* both supernatural and paradisiacal.

In fact, ideology localizes the event, makes it the cornerstone of another world, another society, another humanity. Despite appearances, it rises like a loaf whose leaven comes in two measures, one part cosmology and one part apocalypse. Accordingly, ideology rests on the nostalgia for a beginning of beginnings or on the vision of an end of ends. And of course it is and remains essentially apocalyptic, which explains why it can both resemble and be fiercely opposed to the supernatural apocalypticism so typically characteristic of Christianity in decline.

By contrast with classical myth, dominated as it is by its orientation toward anamnesis, ideology is rather more easily swayed into futurist directions. Still it is not, any more than myth, shaken by the contrary facts of daily life, given its way of transplanting the event into a tradition which soon becomes orthodoxy. By contrast with language, which gives us thereby its utopian dimension, ideology is incapable of admitting its own decay. That is why, too, by comparison with ideology, utopia is less apocalyptic than eschatological, less oriented toward a lost paradise than toward the kingdom.

3. UTOPIA AND ESCHATOLOGY

Ultimately, while ideology articulates an iconoclasm of the real, it is in an iconoclasm of the imaginary itself that utopia finds its source. With ideology, iconoclasm is like lighting a backfire to circumscribe some forest fire; with utopia, it is like a desert reflowering. In the light of ideology, from classless society to valueless ethics, everything afflicts man with visions of another world. By contrast, utopia, like the kingdom, is moved by the vision of a new world, radically other than the "other world" itself. The heart of the matter is this: what can trigger such a vision is not an event which would be either primal or final; it can only be a *novum,* namely, that which nature could not engender nor history give birth to.

While ideology errs by an excess of realism—an excess which may just as easily point to some hypertrophy of idealism—utopia challenges the impossible and seeks to cast the world in the mold of the *novum.* Echoing, as it were, the biblical view of the world as creation, utopia holds that only the *novum* is realizable, everything else being nothing but repetition, nothing but sclerosis. In this respect, no better example can be cited than the church and the gradual thwarting of its utopianism. Through the ages, it abandons the iconoclasm of the imaginary with which it began and, making a travesty of this, its eschatological vocation, settles for a simple iconoclasm of the real, and is led to the impasse of aggiornamentos always lagging behind the *novum.* As it becomes acculturated, the church cannot help shrinking and becoming merely an announcer of the end of the world—hoping, it seems, surreptitiously to survive this end, although quite aware that there will be no church in the New Jerusalem.

But then, the church is also an institution. And it, too, must therefore recognize and suffer from this Achilles' heel of utopia. Apparently, no institution seems appropriate enough to utopia, even if now and then communities try to overlook the matter.

Thus, according to Mannheim, utopia always appears to be divorced from the real. The real seems stiff, it is frozen. It traps man, locking him up in the world and, no less suddenly, locking him out of it. In fact, however, the divorce is only apparent, as is also the absence of institutions. In view of better things *tomorrow,* institutions have simply, as it were, all gone underground. Possibly because the real, always in process and therefore ahead of itself, always lies beyond even fiction, or, on the other hand, possibly because every utopia, if it is hampered by mere fiction and hemmed in, must crumble like a house of cards or be swallowed by the system and turn into ideology. Despite Mannheim, utopia is therefore never severed from the real. And if it sometimes seems to be, this is because utopia, pushing back, so to speak, the boundaries of the real, locates reality beyond the shadows of the real itself, in the very light of the imaginary. Utopia, like any living thing, can degenerate and turn into ideology. It is nevertheless closer to eschatology than to ideology.

While ideology socializes the event, thereby dissolving it into the permanence or persistence of a society, utopia meets it in terms of a dialectic of the imaginary and the real, and consequently conceives of society as parable of a *novum* time and again renewed. In every sense of the term, utopia knows no end; it is a technique, a method of *Weltanschauung,* incapable by definition of reducing the *eschaton* to the *novum*—incapable, too, of making them coincide. Otherwise utopia would have to radicalize the *novum,* and this is the prerogative of eschatology.

Compared to ideology, which "descends," so to speak, from history, utopia tends to get caught up in a perpetual escalation of the future. Eschatology differs from either of them by joining the *eschaton* and the *novum,* and is spared the temptation of utopian overbidding or ideological inflation. Better still, by joining together *eschaton* and *novum,* eschatology is able to vindicate, through an ethic of pleroma, the best that utopia could dream of in its pursuit of pluralism or ideology in its pursuit of universalism, an ethic of the pleroma which, to the extent that iconoclasm is its spearhead, is actually not an ethic of values either.[7] It is the only ethic capable of authorizing both the

---

7. Cf. 1 Cor. 7:22–24: "He who was called in the Lord as a slave is freedman of the Lord. Likewise he who was free when called is a slave of Christ. You were bought with a price; do not become slaves. So, brethren, in whatever state each was called, there let him remain with God"; 1 Cor. 7:29–31: "The appointed

rehabilitation of the imaginary, which ideology wrongs by turning into the museum of a static reality, and the recapitulation of the real, which utopia wrongs in construing it as a hemorrhage of the imaginary.

As a result, compared with the cult of progress fostered by ideology, even the radicalism on which utopia thrives winds up in romanticism. And utopia appears as a tolerance of history: a lucky history, indeed, if only because it is able, at last, somehow to stretch farther than the very servitudes to which, in the meantime, it restricts the human condition.

Ultimately we are once again brought back to man. It would be useless to try to construe the human reality and its framework merely in prospective or merely in retrospective terms. Man, even hemmed in by his body, is a celebration of the spirit, and need not be reduced to some kind of prelude or postlude to the word become flesh: man is neither foreword nor afterword, but the word come into its own. He comes into his own to the extent that God, the wholly other, is articulated through the human reality when, overcoming history, *novum* and *eschaton* united usher in the *kairos,* the pleroma, the fullness of time. Whether or not nature and history converge, man rises, not in the wake of such a convergence, but from word and scripture coming together, from the encounter of the imaginary and the real, from the meeting of flesh and spirit, the *kairos* of the *novum* and of the *eschaton.*

Nature and history, like soteriology, belong to a stream of interpretation different from that of eschatology and utopia, or time.

Much less, then, must utopia be confused with the reign of God. Nor does it, any more than ideology, actually have the power to vest the eschatic dimension of the human reality in some scripture or, even, in some language: the thing happens, and all things are made new only because God alone speaks.

The whole human reality stands or falls with God's speaking. If ideology can do without language, utopia itself cannot, even

---

time has grown very short; from now on, let those who have wives live as though they had none, and those who mourn as though they were not mourning, and those who rejoice as though they were not rejoicing, and those who buy as though they had no goods, and those who deal with the world as though they had no dealings with it. For the form of the world is passing away."

if it sometimes must overstate its case or overreach its point and, given its pluralism, go farther than language dare without exploding.

An eschatological vector of the human reality, language is liable to the pluralism of utopia just as it is exposed to the totalitarian universalism of ideology. Even so, it is and remains our best bastion against both.

4. ESCHATOLOGY AND WORD

Language is the structuring of all human reality as the verbal condition of God. To be sure, such an assertion holds only when language itself holds a line forward of the human reality, just as grace is the forward, eschatological line of sinful man justified. Even so, language shows two sides, one ideological, the other utopian, and both can obstruct or isolate this forward line as well as support it.

Where ideology prevails, language seeks to revert to body language. Postulating the adequacy of the word to the thing, ideology is thus pegged on the supremacy of life lived (if not outlived) and dwarfs every reality under the fallacious pretext that the millennium is imminent. On the other hand, where utopia prevails language grows wings, and there is no telling whether these are the wings of the doves of peace, or of the eagles that nest in every tower of Babel. The *novum* then is realizable, but only once and for all, and language, exiling man, scatters him to the four corners of the world. Admittedly, by contrast with utopia, which can at least be reborn and fly from peak to peak, ideology enjoys no leeway. It must adapt itself to the chores of time and each passing moment, and to the fads that come and go. And, moreover, the utopianism of language is too pluralistic to be satisfied with the onomatopoeiae of the millennium, even if it is driven to concede its dearth as soon as, at the *kairos* of the *novum* and the *eschaton,* the human reality, by reason of its radical integrity, is experienced as attesting to the no less radical otherness of God. At best, then, the utopianism

41

of language serves only to reveal that "it" speaks. What is still lacking is what Saint Paul tried to express when he wrote: "It is no longer I that live, but Christ that lives in me" (Gal. 2:20). And that is why, considering the believer as God's witness, the New Testament calls him a speaker of the spirit and holds that what speaks through him is not "it," but the spirit. Being a new creature means accordingly that it is impossible to reduce life to the outlived, or language to a simple *lapsus ideologiae* intended to reinforce the canonicity of received texts, no more than it is possible to reduce the utopianism of scripture to sempiternal post-scriptum exercises forever forbidden access to the new dawns of the spirit. The language of the *eschaton*, when moreover it also bears the *novum*, points neither to *imitatio* nor to *divinatio*, but to *revelatio*, an articulation of the word made flesh.

Utopia, as has been pointed out, is that which knows no end. Yet it does not really suffer from a lack of meaning. What it lacks is the incarnation. In comparison, ideology overloads language to such an extent that meaning becomes intolerable, except in one direction only. From the standpoint of ideology, language is in fact a kind of measuring stick; it is used to judge. Oddly enough, it condemns, and instead of letting speak, "it" speaks.

5. LANGUAGE AND IDEOLOGY

In the final analysis, it all depends on what purview language comes under. Schematically, if this purview is stated in terms of origin, ideology is the prevailing trend; if it is stated in terms of innovation, utopia is the prevailing trend; only when it is stated in terms of destination, of futurition,[8] are we grappling with eschatology.

The thirst for *archè* from which ideology suffers blinds it to the positive aspects of the futurism that mars the innovation in which utopia glories. And the latter stumbles in its turn when

---

8. Not to be confused with futurism, which is merely the converse of passéism. In futurism, the present is not worth the future. In futurition, the future hangs on whether the present is worth it.

it yields to its tendency to confuse futurism with resurrection. Only an eschatological approach can allow for conceiving language in terms of futurition, that is to say, as prolepsis of the resurrection, *now* of the permanent *novum.*

In like manner, to the extent that it shows a capacity for assigning a sacramental function to language, ideology is equally incapable of resisting clericalism, which is the religious form of totalitarianism or, for that matter, of universalism. As for utopia, swept along by the prophetism characterizing its various charisms, it tends to become blurred in the half-light of pluralism. For these different reasons, we have tried to justify opting for an eschatological concept of language by showing how language, as instrument of pleroma, allows for overcoming the vicissitudes of totalitarianism as well as the tyrannies of pluralism. As a structure of the *eschaton,* language consists only of living cells; by definition, it does not alienate, it can only be liberating. It is at the antipode of the abode of the dead and it lets the dead worry about the dead. Besides, the past as such can never cross the threshold of any language. Raised from the experience of life, language is obliterated unless it can and does prevent experience from surviving itself. It likewise breaks the spell of prophetism, inasmuch as the *eschaton* would, without the *novum,* only be an absolute.

To speak of creation amounts to saying that the *novum* is possible, and to speak of the *eschaton* amounts to saying, in particular, that the *novum* is equally realizable. What is important is not to change the things of this world into a world of things, or to change either nature or history into technology. What is important is to be in this world in such a way that everything has its place, and that there is a time for everything —this world which no word can express except by turning it into creation.

III

The *Eschaton* as *Novum*

1. MAN AND THE TECHNIQUES
OF THE HUMAN

More serious than the divorce between sacred and profane, or the fallacious hostility between religious and secular, more nefarious than the opposition between natural and supernatural, or the simplistic antagonism between Christ and Caesar, is the pernicious way in which the children of this age, squandering their heritage, denounce technology in the name of nature while attacking utopia in the name of history. They forget that even the state of innocence claimed for natural man, as well as the destiny assumed by free man, ultimately seeks only to express that which is the fundamental aspect of the human reality, its utopianism. Innocence and destiny are not mutually exclusive, but converge in utopia.

There is no humanity without technology. The human itself depends on techniques, and utopia is ultimately nothing other than a technique of human technologies just as the imaginary is a technique of the real. Under the guise of a pluralistic secularism, however, this age in which we live appears even more sectarian than the medieval world in all the parochialism of its universalistic pretensions. Nor should this be too surprising.

And we should not be surprised, either, when we realize that contemporary atheism has, in order to quench its thirst for religiosity, found no other source than a paganism left over from Christianity—left over from Christianity if only because by paganism is meant here, not non-Christian religions, but total refusal, absolute negation, unbridled rejection of the utopianism which is at stake even in a rather mystical conception like "life in Christ." The life in Christ is not simply a matter of *imitatio Christi* with Jesus as the model, and hence a focus on the end of the world. The life in Christ is not a matter of a return to the sources, but of a "return of Christ." To live in Christ is not to live one utopia after another, in the retrieval of one utopia after another, but, on the contrary, to *live Christ.* It is to live as that man in whose being is woven the event through which the Word becomes flesh. So much so that God—the one who is, who was, and is to come—is all in all only if he remains radically other, the *eschaton:* that for which man, whose only condition is Christ, through faith is the spokesman.

2. MAN AS LANGUAGE OF HOPE

We can follow Pascal and situate man between two infinites, or Jacques Monod and situate him between chance and necessity. With more or less attention to tradition, we can also understand man in terms of some ability to renew himself in nature or in history as in some kind of elixir of youth. Furthermore, we can even (so to speak) show that he makes his entrance the moment he is caught between an *already* and a *not yet,* between a beginning which would be an end and an end which would similarly be a beginning. In a word, we can situate man between two opposites which, in the final analysis, can only coincide because they annul one another.

But we are following a completely different track when, for example, we find our inspiration in a statement like that of Luther, for whom man is *simul justus ac peccator,* at once justified and a sinner, a sinner who can only believe, a believer who can only confess his sin—such is man. He is, to use an expression now sorely abused, that which he is not and is not that which he is. And we must stress that what transcends man is neither beyond nor on this side of man. What transcends him is *the human.* Neither angel nor beast, this is a reality occurring nowhere except in man since it only occurs in the advent of Christ;

it occurs only through the advent of man as word, a word through which is expressed and confirmed a basically different characteristic of the human reality, its utopianism.

Nothing shakes this utopianism, not even the bankruptcy of language, language which, because it no longer speaks the word, can only serve to suppress the human and to support ideology.

From this point of view, the shift from idea to language in contemporary philosophical reflection is a gain and not a loss, an advantage and not a detriment. For, as I shall try to show, it is above all through language that the utopian dimension of human reality is expressed.

1. Far from constituting a system of identities and differences which are absorbed in one another, of oppositions which cancel out one another, and in which otherness is, in the final analysis, converted to sameness, and hope is reduced to the rank of *déjà vu,* language tips the unsaid into the said. It says something only if what it says is new, is a *novum;* it excludes repetition as well as retrieval. Never blocked by what it says, it opens up the possibility of saying something new; it is an instrument of revelation, insofar as revelation consists not in the cloistering of language but in its openness to the word by which it is grasped, in the incarnation of the word. In other terms, the dialectic of language is geared to utopia, in the same way that the utopianism of the human reality is geared to the incarnation, where God, the radically other, does not stagnate in man inasmuch as man, though nothing but a life already lived, always remains to be lived. And thus the human reality, being that for which God is the radically other rather than an absolute, is liberated from all false utopianism. In particular, it is liberated from the utopianism ultimately engendered by every notion of a *coincidentia oppositorum* whose terms lose and find each other in turn, and stagnate or unfold within one another, driven as they are by all too subtle connivances of mutual eclipse and epiphany.

2. All language calls for utopia. The more a word is adequate to what is meant or lived, the more language is pervaded by utopia, to such an extent that, on the one hand, the catalysis which transforms utopia into living experience in no way consists in outliving language. Language is what integrates man as

a whole. But it does so only if man is thereby realized other than as a body—his own—doomed to death (Rom. 7:24), other than as a life already lived. For language can only be about that which remains to be lived, only about man still to be realized. Otherwise, by way of language, there would be only an ideological system meant to enslave man to that which dooms him to die, or rather to that which *would* doom him to die if the man who ultimately inhabits man existed neither beyond nor on this side of man, in the human. And by the human is of course meant no flight forward, no starry-eyed mysticism, but rather the confrontation with the daily realities through which man is reconciled with his own reality, where heaven and earth, instead of confusing or dissolving one another, are articulated by one another as on the seventh day, the day of rest, or in the Easter dawn of the third day, or in the morning of the fullness of time.

3. In the incarnation, God and man are not interchangeable opposites. Their relationship is one not of opposition but of otherness. It is not God himself who becomes man, but his word which becomes flesh. God thus remains the radically other in relation to man; because of the incarnation, it is not necessary to erase God so that man can affirm himself in all his integrity. The incarnation would not involve God and would be devoid of meaning if it did not allow man, as Pierre Emmanuel would say,[1] to live with himself; if it did not seek to make him a temple of the Spirit rather than enclosing him in some deeper self as in a prison.

3. THE *ESCHATON*: FROM THE APOCALYPTIC OF THE SACRED TO ESCHATOLOGICAL UTOPIANISM

At this point, a new vision of the sacred is emerging and it cannot help but both surprise and comfort us: surprise us, for

---

1. Pierre Emmanuel, "La dimension négligée," *Le Monde,* 12 February 1973.

the liberation of man seems inconceivable today unless it reinforces one or the other of the multiple factors of desacralization which gluts contemporary civilization; comfort us, for even if technology is not conducive to the sacred as traditionally defined, it is not, despite appearances, prevented from providing the sacred with a relevance more significant than that imposed by our traditional dualisms, or by the monism with which we oppose them. Indeed, what is the sacred if not a religious metaphor, an existential onomatopoeia designating the radically other, in terms of which man dwells in man? The sacred is concerned less with man coming to terms with the natural, or its antonym the supernatural, than with the essentially utopian character of the human reality. Nor does traditional theology ignore this. To the extent that it proclaims vigorously that God alone is holy, what can it mean except that God is neither being nor nonbeing but the radically other, in terms of which man is that which he is not and is not that which he is? Furthermore, is it not true that existence is only a problem for man and not for God? Kierkegaard and, later, Tillich were not mistaken on this point when they willingly admitted that it would be improper to say of God that he exists. Let us also recall what Jesus himself declares: "Verily, verily, I say unto you: he who receives the one whom I send receives me and who receives me receives the one who sent me" (John 13:20); and Jesus adds, as if to avoid all misunderstanding, "My word is not mine, it is the word of the one who sent me" (John 14:24).

I am perfectly willing, then, to agree with those who say that our civilization has lost its sense of the sacred. This loss is undoubtedly real—but only in a very particular sense, dependent upon one conception of the sacred *among others*. Nor must we conceal, ultimately, that this loss is real and true only for those who are one culture behind, those for whom the sacred in fact only serves to compensate for another loss, that of the earthly paradise. The sacred is lost only if one still tries to hold on to a culture impregnated with the supernatural, where the sacred is in some way a consolation for a lost paradise, but also, we should stress, where it therefore is only a negative utopianism: negative because it is focused, not on the idea of *novum*, but on the idea of *initium*, not on the renewal of all created things,

but on a primal myth, not on the notion of creation as steward-
ship of nature, but on the notion of nature as residue of demiurgic activity. Thus, to the extent that the sacred corresponds to
a concrete dimension of the human reality, the loss of the sacred
today reveals the necessity of rethinking the sacred in terms of
its even more intimate and hence primordial meaning as the
utopian arena of transcendence. This necessity confronts us all
the more ineluctably since it emerges, not simply at random, but
in keeping with the most profound exigencies of technological
civilization, above all with the positive utopianism which constitutes its true matrix.

We will have the opportunity to return to this problem of the
sacred and the particular aspects it acquires in the context of
technological civilization. We will then attempt to demonstrate
how the dialectic of the profane and the sacred is in reality a
question of the transcendence of God, and how technological
utopianism is in this respect the heir of that dialectic. But the
same causes produce the same effects; let us be satisfied for the
moment with pointing out how great is the poverty of the sacred
though this poverty is obscured by the vehemence with which
the sacred is invoked to attack the utopianism of technological
civilization.

In this regard, one needs only ponder again the quotation
from Berdyaev which appears as the epigraph to Aldous Huxley's *Brave New World:* "Utopias appear far more realizable than
we once thought. And we currently find ourselves before a
question anguishing in a far different sense: How do we avoid
their definitive realization? Utopias are realizable. Life marches
on toward utopias. And perhaps a new century is beginning, a
century where intellectuals and the cultivated classes will dream
of means to avoid utopias and to return to a non-utopian society, less 'perfect' and more free."[2]

Confronted as we are with an equally realizable and therefore
no less inevitable apocalypse, Berdyaev's warning undoubtedly
includes a protest which is still relevant.

It seems, nevertheless, that Berdyaev was mistaken on one
essential point, that he even committed a double error. Apart

2. Aldous Huxley, *Brave New World* (Harper & Row, New York, 1932).

from the fact that he unjustly forces us to choose between lost paradise and apocalypse, in other words, between two negative forms of utopia, two counter-utopias, his thought stops short of acknowledging any positive forms of utopia whatever. Referring as he does to a society "less perfect and more free," Berdyaev does not acknowledge, or at least does not see, that there has been no social structure which was not at the same time a bridge between the imaginary and the real. He fails to acknowledge that, like existence, utopia precedes structure. Worse still, he does not accept the fact that utopia is equally antithetical to lost paradise and to apocalypse. Let me clarify this.

1. Just as it is through language that man transcends the mute horizon of his body, it is by virtue of utopianism that man adheres to his own humanity and is integrated into the community of men. As is the case with language, the social structure does not so much institute as constitute utopia: it calls for utopia.

Far from inciting us to evade the world, utopia invites us to cast anchor there, and does so regardless of the nature of the particular problematic found at its base. Proof of this is found in all cosmologies in which man slakes his thirst for knowledge as soon as he is spurred on by even haphazardly organized elements of any new problematic. A similar proof can likewise be found in the common notion that because *a* world nears its end, the end of *the* world is imminent.

Utopia, which is thus distinguished as much from apocalypse as from ideology, does not overwhelm the imaginary with the real, nor does it sublimate the real in the imaginary. At its very heart a twofold element prevents utopia from succumbing to any deviation, whether apocalyptic or ideological. This question is, namely, whether or not the vision of a new world glimpsed by utopia is both possible and realizable, and moreover whether or not what we are talking about is really a new world. It is not enough for this vision to be vaguely irresistible; it must still be based on some technique. Failing this, the utter gratuity of the vision takes precedence over its efficacy and, just as quickly, mystique over reality. Is it not, precisely, the error of every marginal community to attempt to change man by making him change worlds, as if in this way one could more easily succeed in changing one's life?

It is true that these marginal communities are not the only ones denouncing technology. Quite involuntarily, perhaps, they restrict themselves to reflecting in their options the opinions unhesitatingly formulated by every orthodox thinker who condemns technology on the grounds that it is simply a machine meant only to produce more efficiency. However, I am not sure that efficiency is in itself a vice. Nor am I so sure that those who most loudly denounce waste and garbage are not also the ones who profit by our consumer society. To be sure, in other ages man did become accustomed to the idea that nature abhors a vacuum or that grace is, at the least, efficacious. No, it is not technology that we must distrust, much less the efficiency with which we charge it, and to which we accuse it of succumbing.

Of course, whoever seeks only to compensate for the deficiencies of the real is already victim of a pseudo-technology whose fascination will sooner or later trap him by offering him both therapy and salvation.

But we must not confuse such compensatory techniques, techniques which even prayer has not always been able to resist,[3] with the problematic proper to what is being referred to as technological civilization. Risking a cliché, one might say that there is technique and there is technique. The one whose worth we seek to disclose finds its norm, not in a compensatory imagination emerging from the deficiencies of the real, but in the imaginary which fulfills the real, inasmuch as the real is not to be confused with either nature or history. Of course, technology does offend our traditional sensibilities. But, over against this offense, it affords a certain advantage, that is, it does not fall into the snare of classical thought, which tends to regard man as a vacuum, a lack filled by nature, a freedom seduced by history.

Indeed, both nature and history can just as easily overwhelm the real as constitute its matrix. They can and in fact do shortcircuit it, precisely to the extent that for both the real is only the

---

3. Cf. the words of Jesus to those who only know how to repeat unceasingly, "Lord, Lord" (Matt. 7:21).

ineluctable, to the extent that both consider as possible only what is necessary.

2. It is thus a question of not betraying the real. But then, if we want to avoid subjecting the real to any deterministic system, above all we must refrain from violating its inherent utopianism. We must reject the misshapen images of utopianism which both history and nature engender as they offer themselves as matrices of both the real and the human reality. We must not be taken in. Instead, we must begin by asking ourselves, in particular since by nature man is estranged from himself, whether he is not destined by his own nature to something other than "nature." Indeed, is this not the question already raised from the mythological perspective—if we are to believe Eliade—when history is denounced as a fall and hence considered a process that must be resisted and ultimately rejected? There is no dearth of authors for whom, all things considered, myth reflects an ahistorical if not anti-historical reading of human reality.

History, like nature, can also estrange man from himself; it too can be dehumanizing. The proof of this is that man does not hesitate, whatever the cost, to endow history with a messianic goal which in reality merely endorses failure. At one point, it is the road to freedom terminating in a cul-de-sac; at another, it is the feeling that in a system totally geared to becoming, there is no human reality which does not prove in the final analysis to be a useless passion.

And yet we will hear this objection: Is it not in terms of the supernatural that, not without reason, the real meaning of nature was thought to be defined? Likewise, is it not in terms of the eschatological that scattered fragments of history were gathered together into a history? Yes, but precisely on condition that we refrain from deciphering the human in such a way as to turn it into a mere process of initiation which, taking its cue from a dialectic of *initium* and *finis,* would move, so to speak, *from* the natural *to* the supernatural. Yes again, but on condition that we refrain from construing the human in such a way as to turn it into a mere apocalyptic process which, by taking its cue from the dialectic of *already* and *not yet,* would move, so to speak, *from* the historical *to* the eschatological. Yes, finally, if we perceive the dialectic of the natural and the supernatural, the historical and the eschatological, in such a way that it mediates a transcendence which, imbued though it is with quite a sacral significance, remains no less pervaded by the irreducible utopianism of its significations.

4. THE *NOVUM*

In reality, nature has no end of surprises for us. Even when we assimilate it in a blind series of repetitions, it still confronts us as chance.

History is no different; it weighs on us. In thus making us bear all the aphasic burden of the past, history determines us—but in such a way that sometimes fate seems to want to link us to a destiny, or rather to that which is able to assert itself as freedom, incarnating the futurable dimension as well as representing the ethical demand consistent with that destiny.

But, for all this, it certainly does not follow that we are protected from a kind of immanentism which, although it avoids drifting openly into apocalypticism, nevertheless does not open onto the eschatological, or which, in repressing the eschatological, is likewise hostile to utopia. By different paths, whether through "chance" or through fate, or perhaps because of their respective logic, nature and history are still too frail not to give way to the dialectic of identity and difference, of the other and the same. Moreover, the very imperialism of such a dialectic also reveals its defect. Indeed, what this dialectic lacks is precisely what is missing in the logic of "chance" as well as in the logic of fate, namely, what happens when dressed-up nature tips over into creation, and redressed history tips over into destiny: the *novum*.

If we had to begin by saying what the *novum* is not, we would say it is not what takes place when, at the risk of distorting necessity, nature or history appear to open up on some novelty, on some kind of automatic miracle in relation to which either God would only be superfluous or, eventually, confused with

53

nature (a confusion eloquently attested to by the *deus sive natura* of a tradition reborn each time man seems to reach an impasse); or, history would be confused with *gesta dei* (a confusion feeding all kinds of messianism gone stale). Creation and destiny would then be the *terminus ad quem* respectively of nature and of history; they would be the ineluctable mouthpiece of an automatism of one sort or another.

Against such opinions, we subscribe to the biblical argument for which God, the creative word, enters the web of both nature and history, assuming them in the act of his creation and destination. Accordingly, we must consider nature in view of creation, and history in view of destiny (or redemption), not the converse. As the respective arenas of creation and destiny, both nature and history are thus liberated from the cycles as well as the finalities in which the determinisms afflicting them tend to imprison them. And for the same reasons nature and history are at once God's handiwork and man's masterwork, like Canaan when Israel established itself there as in the Promised Land, or like sacred history de-divinized by the destiny of Israel until it became the history of Jesus, and of every man whose destiny lies in God inasmuch as such a destiny includes man.

I thus call *novum* the advent of man as the human, man as the event of God, even while God remains the radically other. I call *novum* not only man but the human; steeped in nature as man is, and molded by history, the human is nonetheless experienced as totally other than nature, history, and, for that matter, all human techniques. Apart from the fact that the *novum* encompasses not only man but also the human, it also encompasses what is alien to man: it is what happens to man when the human is the event of God. Accordingly, the *novum* is to the *eschaton* as man is to God; and, likewise the *eschaton,* in relation to the *novum,* signifies that which, being radically other, is God in relation to man, a relation which it eludes only by converting it to the greatness of man.

The *novum* is thus caught sight of in man's own vocation. It points to the way in which man assumes his responsibility to humanize the order of things by liberating it, whether from the chronological, the biological, or the artificial. For the sake of both clarity and simplicity, let us point out that what Qoheleth understands as *novum* is, indifferently, the world taken either as nature or history, or as neither one nor the other; and what he understands as world is that which results from a technique of the human. Thus he can write: "Go, eat your bread with enjoyment, and drink your wine with a merry heart; for God has already approved what you do. Let your garments be always white; let not oil be lacking on your head. Enjoy life with the wife whom you love, all the days of your vain life which he has given you under the sun, because that is your portion in life and in your toil at which you toil under the sun. Whatever your hand finds to do, do it with your might; for there is no work or thought or knowledge or wisdom *in Sheol,* to which you are going" (Eccles. 9:7–10).[4]

If only we consider this passage in its context, it is obvious that, on the one hand, Qoheleth views the *novum* less in terms of a fate which man could not escape than in terms of a destiny which is proper to him and which he must manage, and that, on the other hand, the *novum* must no more be thought of in terms of Sheol than the return of Christ in terms of the apocalypse.[5] The *novum* no more forces man to resign himself to the "end of the world" than it rivets his gaze to the rearview mirror of the contrasting myth of the *initium,* the origin of origins.

The *novum* remains linked to the problem of the *eschaton,* which is its native ground. And it is in order better to survey, or rather, better to sense this relation that we propose to sketch a definition of eschatology against the background of the associated problem of utopia. For as Isaiah declares in the supplication of Hezekiah, the king of Judea:

> For Sheol cannot thank thee,
>   death cannot praise thee;
> those who go down in the pit cannot hope
>   for thy faithfulness.
> The living, the living, he thanks thee,
>   as I do this day;

---

4. Italics added.
5. Cf. Jürgen Moltmann, *The Crucified God* (Harper & Row, New York, 1974), p. 21.

the father makes known to the children
thy faithfulness.
The Lord will save me,
and we will sing to stringed instruments
all the days of our life,
at the house of the Lord. (Isa. 38:18–20)

IV

Eschatology and Technological Utopianism

1. ESCHATOLOGY AND PLEROMA

A. From Soteriological to Sacramental Eschatology

In order to situate the argument which follows and to get a better bearing on our undertaking, it is perhaps worthwhile to begin by indicating what, in our opinion, are the characteristic features of trinitarian eschatology as handed down to us in the Christian tradition. This will allow us to highlight the two perspectives, soteriological and sacramental, which make up our argument.

First of all, let us consider the three types of trinitarian eschatology.

We easily recognize each of them by its dominant trait, which is focused in such a way that it favors one of the persons of the trinity: Father, Son, or Holy Spirit. Depending upon its dominant trait, each of these three types possesses its own leitmotiv. Thus, an eschatology in which the Father has primacy will be oriented toward the *other world,* a world whose hour will come when, in conformity with the origin and the meaning of its original creation, the restoration of this fallen world will be completed. At the same time, an eschatology in which the role of the Son predominates will be focused on the *reconversion of the world* according to a process whose twofold theme expresses the idea that God bodies forth as man so that man may body forth as God. Finally, in an eschatology governed by the Spirit, it seems that the central theme will always deal with the *end of the world.*

I know the risk I run in thus presenting a threefold simplification that some will judge too extreme. I will venture, nevertheless, to cite as representative of the first type Saint Irenaeus, for his theory of recapitulation, and Saint Thomas, for his conception of the beatific vision of God. As representative of the second type I do not hesitate to mention Saint Augustine, on the one hand, for his conception of the incarnation as the link between the city of God and the terrestrial city, and Calvin, on the other hand, for his way of understanding the reign of Christ as extending, not only over the government of the church, but also over the government of man, over politics. As far as the third type is concerned, its most worthy representatives run from Joachim of Fiore to those Anabaptists of the sixteenth century who attempted the ultimate experiment of radicalizing the Reformation. For the latter, as for Joachim of Fiore, the age of the Spirit constitutes in some way the estuary of both the age of the Father and the age of the Son.

These three types, let us repeat, are characterized by a common tendency to conceive the *eschaton*[1] as a manifesto now of the Father, now of the Son, and now of the Spirit. We will not, however, go so far as to pretend that in moving from one type to the other we commit the error of "periodizing" the *eschaton,* that is to say, of partitioning it by dividing it into as many periods as there are persons in the trinity, or into as many phases as there are stages in salvation. Nonetheless, the three

---

1. In *classical* theology, eschatology is concerned with the doctrine of the last things, the ultimate reality *(eschaton)* of man; the latter will be revealed in all its glory in the bosom of God, when God will be all in all. It is not an accomplishment which emanates from man's possibilities; but then, for this very reason, man is the one who is concerned. The incarnation constitutes the first fruits of this ultimate reality, just as creation is its ground. It is also, then, a truth which in a way is *already* revealed even if man does *not yet* enjoy it fully.

The *eschaton* is different from the *arche* (principle) which designates the principle of all things at the beginning of beginnings, and which, especially in mythological antiquity, designates the principle in relation to which nothing is that is not fallen.

One immediately sees the difference; from the point of view of the *eschaton,* all is promise.

types of eschatology we have just pointed out are not entirely free from suspicion.

And it is not without justification that this is the case. Even with Joachim of Fiore, who develops an evolutionary conception of the trinity (though at first in a tolerable way), the tendency to apportion the *eschaton* in terms of periods proper to the Father, the Son, and the Holy Spirit becomes truly embarrassing when it reverberates at the level of salvation. In the final analysis, one cannot assign different periods to the different persons of the trinity without running the risk of fragmenting the *eschaton,* apportioning it before weaving it into the various stages and periods involving salvation.

Where the notion of history predominates, we witness the fragmentation of the trinity. Where the notion of salvation predominates, we witness the historicization of eschatology. And what we are dealing with is a soteriological "periodization."

Whatever the infraction incurred by this tendency, it in no way alters the reading which we first suggested in comparing these three types of eschatology. Nothing stops us from highlighting what they have in common, and which, moreover, characterizes the Christian tradition in general until the present day. This common theme refers to the notion, a very special one, of salvation as that which grants us access to history—better still, as that which is offered to us in the very unfolding of history.

Yet it remains true that this soteriological "periodization" is nothing but the secret of an eschatology with trinitarian markings, no matter which trait prevails or which type results from it. From one type to another, whether obviously or surreptitiously, the *eschaton* is conceived of in terms of a dialectic that scarcely varies, recognizable in that it oscillates between two poles, the *already* and the *not yet,* this world and the next. In terms of salvation, it is obvious that this way of structuring the dialectic of the *eschaton* affords definite advantages. Assured of his salvation, man lives in the hope of a life hereafter, the only life with a future. The disadvantages, however, are no less obvious when we consider the existence of the believer and see the reality of the new man from the viewpoint of the reign of God;

59

in the expectation of a future life, the believer is in the mean-time driven to live in two different worlds.

By raising against any soteriological periodization the objection that it fixes the dialectic of the *eschaton* between an *already* and a *not yet*, we are accusing it of reducing this dialectic to a single dimension of history; in short, we are blaming it for historicizing eschatology. It matters little in the end whether this dimension of history is only one among many (as with theologians who preach the secularization or the politicization of faith), or whether it is the true dimension of history, its hidden face (as with theologians who conceive the natural exclusively as something taken over by the supernatural or history solely as an arena for God's design). As far as we are concerned, such historicization of eschatology inevitably debilitates the dialectic of the *eschaton,* for the simple reason that it attenuates the very utopianism by means of which the *eschaton* constitutes its structure.

At the risk of becoming colloquial, we can say that the historicization of eschatology results in the transformation of the *eschaton* into apocalypse fiction, in the same way as utopia, at least in the eyes of its detractors, can be characterized as an outlandish science fiction of the unrealizable. But to return to theology: this debilitation of eschatology to the point of senescence is the inevitable outcome, equally for those for whom faith is reduced to a desperate pursuit of hope as a flight into the future[2] and for those for whom hope is explained by the fact that today, *post mortem dei,* faith can only be reduced to silence.[3]

Perhaps because it caters to its affliction, the Christian faith succeeds only in aggravating its obsolescence when it gives in to the multiple solicitations of which it is the object or, more pointedly, by which it is bludgeoned on all sides, whether in the name of some Christological futurism or some divine apophatism.[4] In surrendering to such solicitations faith legitimates a

---

2. For example, among the imitators of Moltmann, rather than Moltmann himself in his *Theology of Hope.*
3. For example, certain aspects of Jacques Ellul, *Hope in Time of Abandonment* (Seabury Press, New York, 1973).
4. André Neher, *L'exil de la parole* (Editions du Seuil, Paris, 1970), gives us one of the clearest examples of this, an example bearing the seal of prophetic Judaism.

false alternative, thereby altering the dilemma which (for the unbeliever and above all for the believer) prevents faith in God from being taken for granted, a dilemma the believer overcomes only by confessing his unbelief (Mark 9:24). What the believer awaits is not the end of the world, but the "return of Christ," and his hope lies not in a God who returns from exile, but in a God who comes (Rev. 1:4), a God whose word becomes flesh. Such a God does not need to be protected from atheism, as we wait for him finally to unveil himself; he is our contemporary. And he is our contemporary not only by virtue of our capacity to hope but also, in particular, by reason of our very incapacity to believe, our unbelief. No one truly expects the kingdom of God unless, when it arrives, he confesses that he is not expecting it; Easter, the zenith of hope, is not a simple outcome of Good Friday, the nadir of unbelief.

We should not be mistaken about the resurrection to the point of confusing it with a kind of wavering hope. Not only unbelief is implicated in the resurrection, but hope as well. Far from marking a simple shift from the first to the second, or even a mutation, the resurrection occurs as the iconoclasm of hope as well as of unbelief; both need to be constantly challenged. Is not this twofold challenge precisely what faith calls for when it claims to be *eschatic* existence, that is, an existence wherein the experience of the human reality is constituted, not by what would simply prolong life, but by what changes it?

When Saint John defines faith as a victory over the world (1 John 5:3), he certainly does not intend this victory to be taken as a figure of speech, employed with the sole purpose of ratifying some Christological futurism, much less any divine apophatism. With all due respect to Bultmann, Saint John is doing something quite different here from yielding to some predominantly cultic tendency. Bultmann is surely mistaken when he accuses the evangelist of sacramentalizing the eschatological tension that characterizes the essential thrust of Jesus' proclamation.[5] For John, the sacrament is neither a futuristic loophole nor an apophatic epiphany. When the author of the Fourth

---

5. Rudolf Bultmann, *The Gospel of John: A Commentary* (Westminster Press, Philadelphia, 1971).

Gospel refers to sacrament, it is solely with the intention of both sustaining and reinforcing the legitimacy of the point of contact he sees between the eschatological dimension of the word become flesh and the utopianism of the verbal condition proper to man, or between eschatology and utopia. In short, by means of the sacrament, Saint John radicalizes the *eschaton,* raising an obstacle in the path of its historicization. He directly counters the idea according to which the *eschaton* would be nothing but an over-determination of history just as in the Middle Ages the supernatural is of the natural.

From such a perspective the following observation, borrowed from Karl Barth, becomes especially pertinent. Never, he says, must we understand *eschaton* simply as "the continuation, the result, the consequence, the next step after the next to last"; on the contrary, it must be understood as "a radical break with everything next to last; and this is just the secret of its moving power."[6] The cross and resurrection of Christ are not meant to defer the advent of the *novum* to the end of the world. The coming of Christ would then have the effect only of dislocating faith and hope, of isolating them from one another. In Christ, on the contrary, the only one who can hope is he who, having eyes to see, sees and yet believes, he who, having ears to hear, hears and yet believes. This is why, symbolically speaking, the believer, rather than awaiting the end of the world, anticipates the "return" of Christ here and now. The "return" of Christ not only means that the *eschaton* depends neither on history nor on nature, nor on anything next to last; it also means that thereby according to their respective aptitude each becomes its arena, a *novum.* By virtue of the *eschaton*—which for Bultmann signifies the cross and resurrection of Christ[7]—in the coming of man to faith here and now, the *novum* bursts forth: into love where alienation reigns, into hope where determinism reigns, into faith where necessity reigns. What heretofore has never arisen in the heart of man now becomes realizable (1 Cor. 2:9). Or,

6. Karl Barth, *Parole de Dieu et parole humaine* (Je sers, Paris, 1933), p. 87.
7. Rudolf Bultmann, "New Testament and Mythology," in *Kerygma and Myth* I, ed. by H. W. Bartsch (S.P.C.K., 1953), sec. II B.

rather, to the criminal crucified with him who told him, "Remember me when you come into your kingdom," Jesus answers, "Truly, I say to you, today you will be with me in paradise" (Luke 23:41–43).

B. The Advent of Christ and Faith as Eschatic Existence

How then are we to understand the *eschaton?* And what is the real meaning, consequently, of faith as eschatic existence?

In answer to the *first* question, let us begin by stressing that, according to biblical thought, the behavior of man is best described in terms of hope. We should add also that this description applies equally to the believer and to the unbeliever: "For this law that I enjoin on you this day is not beyond your strength, or beyond your reach. It is not in heaven, so that you need to wonder, 'Who will go up to heaven for us and bring it down to us, so that we may hear it and keep it?' Nor is it beyond the seas, so that you need to wonder, 'Who will cross the seas for us and bring it back to us, so that we may hear it and keep it?' No, the word is very near to you; it is in your mouth and in your heart, for your observance" (Deut. 30:11–14). Whether from a mythological, "scientific," biological, or spiritual point of view, if we had to reduce man to a single element, it would be hope; indeed, hope is man's only certainty. It is the same Job who, crying out, "He breaks me down on every side, and I am gone, and my hope he pulled up like a tree" (Job 19:10), also adds: "For I know that my Redeemer lives, and at last he will stand upon the earth" (Job 19:25).

But this is not a hope that wavers with the whims of the successive devaluations of man. It is, on the contrary, a hope which constantly holds man up to man as well as up to God. Just this is what the *eschaton* is all about: it moors hope to faith, but without confusing the two. Above all, it prevents hope from selling itself short by fleeing into the future while withholding faith. He alone hopes, we have said, who sees and yet believes: such as the one who awaits the reign of God and his justice, and encounters them in the figure of Christ, such as Simeon, "looking for the consolation of Israel" (Luke 2:25), who cries out facing Christ:

> *Lord, now lettest thou thy servant depart in peace,*
> *according to thy word;*
> *for mine eyes have seen thy salvation*
> *which thou hast prepared in the presence of all peoples,*
> *a light for revelation to the Gentiles,*
> *and for glory to thy people Israel.* (Luke 2:29–32)

We have only one more clarification to make and we will have answered the first question. The *eschaton,* even if it appears in the figure of Christ, does not reduce the coming Christ to the historical Jesus. And, as we have already emphasized, it does not, either, permit us to confuse the "return" of Christ with the "next to last" event par excellence (so to speak) which the notion of the end of the world represents. But it does not send *us* back to Jesus. The most we can say is that it harks back to Jesus, but only to the extent, precisely, that Jesus is a man, like all those for whom, because they hope, God is a contemporary. Against the logic of the New Testament, we make the mistake of believing that faith makes us contemporary with Jesus. Would not Simeon then have preferred to remain rather than to leave in peace, just as at the transfiguration the disciples wished to linger who, having thus missed the point, immediately felt guilty, out of step, as they "[lifted] up their eyes [and] saw no one, but Jesus only" (Matt. 17:1–8; Mark 9:2–8; Luke 9:28–26)?

Just as with creation it is not a question of a process of hominization but of humanizing man and his environment, so with the incarnation there is no question of any kind of hominization of God aiming at a corresponding divinization of man; what is at stake, rather, is the destiny of man acceding to a new quality of the human.

We can now broach the *second* question, namely, the meaning of faith as eschatic existence. In the light of what we have just said concerning the threefold eruption of the *novum* into faith, hope, and love, we are now in a position to point out that its object, the world, belongs only to him who does not covet it.

64

Thus, for Bultmann, the ultimate ramification of his conception of the *eschaton* brings him to describe faith, the reality of the new man, as a kind of process of "de-secularization," a liberation of man from the world, from everything which impedes his extrinsic authenticity. Likewise, for Barth, the irruption of the *eschaton* provokes an analogous process of dehistoricization or, in other words, a liberation of man from everything which impedes his intrinsic authenticity, from history in general and culture in particular. (Indeed, let us not forget that the Christological concentration ordinarily attributed to Barth does not culminate in some cultural elitism which would have put the Swiss theologian into the same camp as Schleiermacher; it culminates in a conception of scripture as a protest against all that is written and which, because it is written, is but a received text.)

In short, the *eschaton* is viewed by Bultmann in terms of desecularization, while in Barth it is viewed as dehistoricization. Whereas Bultmann puts the accent on the desacralization of nature and the world (in order to restore the world to its proper worldliness), Barth emphasizes the desacralization of history and of everything that serves as vehicle of *anagke,* of *fatum* (in order to restore history to its real destiny). Neither Barth nor Bultmann, it goes without saying, succumbs to the tendency which consists in overestimating faith at the expense of hope and love, or of overestimating love at the expense of faith and hope.

In the first tendency, we recognize the so-called realized eschatology school, where the emphasis falls on the *already* which is constituted by the advent of Christ, as if faith consisted more in *reclaiming* Jesus rather than in *proclaiming* Christ in view of our own cultural situation today.

The second tendency is the one manifested by a futuristic eschatology, either because it yields to a triumphalism of glory whose premises drive it to assimilate the return of Christ to a simple end of the world, or—as the super-futurism of a certain contemporary "elpidism"[8] demonstrates—because it succumbs to an inverse triumphalism of the cross and assimilates the

---

8. "Elpidism" is derived from a Greek word, *elpis,* which means hope, and refers to hope based on any indiscriminate motive.

return of Christ, if not to the end of the world, at least to the end of *my* world. In neither case is it taken into account that futurism constitutes the ultimate temptation of utopianism, and this in the face of the realities of a world more and more ineluctable.

As for the third tendency, we find it at work in the *realizing* eschatology which, to cite only a few examples, serves the enthusiasts and other spirituals of the past just as easily as the charismatic movements of today. From one extreme to the other, either the *novum* is dissolved in this world or else it is dissipated in the other world, while the *eschaton* proves almost as transient as the real.

To be sure, we would be wrong to ignore the positive element running through each of these tendencies along which Christian thought has patiently sought to develop itself. We must draw attention to this element, if only to better point out the archeological utopianism which characterizes ancient thought. The major difference lies in the fact that in the utopianism of the *arche,* the *novum* is only the hidden face of necessity, of the *ultima ratio,* and hence is confused with the order of things. By contrast, in the utopianism of the *eschaton* the *novum* has no hegemony except that which, conferred upon it by its utter contingency, is revealed in the things God prepares for those who love him—and these are all things "which no eye has seen, nor ear heard" (1 Cor. 2:9). This, moreover, is why without faith hope itself is useless, and why, without faith and hope, love— which Saint Paul considers the greatest of the three (1 Cor. 13:13)—would soon resemble (as in the surprise-free future of some technocrat) the surprise-free altruism of Dostoyevsky's Grand Inquisitor, an altruism whose ultimate efficiency is the depersonalization of those who fall under its yoke. In order to believe that the kingdom has arrived, it is not enough simply to rechristen Babylon.[9] Indeed, what point would there be in replacing a supra-terrestrial eschatology with a post-terrestrial one, if it must ultimately culminate in a simple ideology of the *novum,* whether its model be the Grand Inquisitor or the tower of Babel? Ernst Bloch is right. While Platonic anamnesis elimi-

---

9. Ernst Bloch, *Man on His Own* (Herder and Herder, New York, 1970) p. 125.

nates all possibility of the *novum*[10] by returning it to the *initium*, a realized teleology does no less violence to the contingency of the *novum*. Indeed, its sovereignty, for being charismatic, can be assured only by the *eschaton*, although on this point one should avoid following the example of the Christian tradition. The latter, by anchoring the dialectic of the *eschaton* to the *initium* of the *already* and to the *not yet* of the *telos*, runs the risk of turning it into an ideology (precisely the one which culminates in the death of God and which, not without reason, contemporary thought challenges). In other words, neither anamnesis nor teleology can prevent itself, each in its own way, from returning the *novum* to an origin of origins or an end of ends. This being so, and if, moreover, we must view the *novum* in the light of the *eschaton*, I do not see how we can possibly do it satisfactorily by approaching the problematic of the *eschaton* from the perspective of a dialectic oscillating between the two poles of lost paradise and apocalypse, poles whose variations, on different levels and in their respective fields, have exercised their power of attraction on the imagination of Western man. Ordinarily, these poles are indicative of dualities, ranging all the way from Eros and Thanatos to being and nonbeing (not to mention "the same and the other"). But the common denominator of these dualities consists in the Leibnizian notion of the best of all possible worlds, a notion already prepared for in the Cartesian dualism of thought and extension. Moreover, this notion, through its underlying immanentism and to the extent that it ultimately warrants what is at stake for theodicy, reflects an approach whose significance acquires its true meaning only in a prerequisite which calls for the very negation of utopia. With different motives and no doubt on different grounds, we ought nonetheless to ask ourselves at this point, like Tertullian: What is there in common between the New Jerusalem and the best of all possible worlds, between utopia and ideology, whether soteriological or not? To be sure, it is conceivable that, out of a desire not to banish transcendence, we agree to sink God in man. But we must acknowledge that such a procedure, which consists at first in a kind of role inversion, is required by its own logic to

---

10. Ibid., p. 82.

develop itself and, ineluctably, to expand in terms of a leveling down of transcendence for the sake of immanence. In short, we must acknowledge that such a procedure results initially in the systematic erosion regardless of the poles involved of one of the terms for the sake of the other, and ultimately in the replacement of iconoclasm by the class struggle or the conflict of generations and the replacement of eschatology by teleology or by anamnesis.

C. Creation and Pleroma

(1) The Radically Other

It is solely with the advent of the *eschaton* that the *novum* can burst forth. Without the *eschaton* there is no *novum,* nor is there utopia without eschatology. As Karl Barth points out, without the creative otherness of God there can be no *novitas mundi.* There would be no possibility for a novation of the world. The *novitas mundi* means precisely that the world in itself can have no meaning since it has a beginning, and consequently that it is the *contingency* of the creator himself which is in question in the very question of this *novitas.* Even Saint Thomas treats it no differently when he deals with this subject, in spite of the fact that his thought submits to norms decreed by natural theology.[11]

In relation to Greek philosophy, biblical thought innovates when it introduces the notion of a creator God. And no longer is God the problem, but man. What is radically iconoclastic in the notion of a creator God is the implication that the creature is creature only on condition that, when called into question, he can resort to no loophole: whether it be, for example, the feeling of absolute dependence whose problematic would be resolved with an affirmation of the existence of God; or the *novitas mundi* itself, if in order to assure the contingency of the creator, it were necessary for the world to be eternal, though only logically; or, if in order to assure this same contingency of God on the level of providence, it were likewise necessary for the world

---

11. Barth, *Church Dogmatics,* III/1, sec. 40, p.4.

to be perfect, even though in a very relative manner. In any case, it should be a cause for concern that we are no longer dealing with the creature, with the very condition of the *novitas* proper to both man and the reality of the world.

Clearly, then, this *novitas* can have meaning only in terms of a radicalization of the very notion of God. How can this radicalization take place? Through the idea of a creator God. The whole problematic of the *novum* is then modified to such an extent that it necessarily passes through the crucible of a radically iconoclastic eschatology. Otherwise, we would constantly come up against a contradiction in terms. God would be only a prolongation of man or his presupposition, an absolute or a simple hypothesis; otherwise we would be dealing with a projection in which God and man would either be opposites or—and for the same reasons—corollaries of one another, unless they were mutually exclusive. Under these conditions, how could anything else exist alongside God? How could the affirmation of such a God not bear with it the very negation of man? In order for man to exist, is it enough to deduce and to affirm that God is, or even that he is dead? Those are so many false questions to which we must respond if we hope finally to silence them. And it is precisely those questions which the radicalization of God addresses in the notion of creation, a notion which in one stroke shifts the reality of man from the realm of nature or history to that of eschatology.

Whether he descends from the ape or from Abraham, man is man only insofar as he is son of God, insofar as he is new man, a citizen not only of earth (in his utopian dimension) but also of heaven (in his eschatic reality). An iconoclastic eschatology embracing the threefold notion of creation, redemption, and pleroma consequently insists on the impossibility of confusing God with nature *(deus sive natura),* of structuring existence on the basis of a feeling of absolute dependence (like Schleiermacher), or of dissolving this triple relation into a pre-established harmony (like Leibniz), as if the world in itself—in the same way as, formerly, the world beyond—were the best expression of God. Not that an iconoclastic eschatology essentially implies the denial that the reality of God could ever be in harmony with the reality of the world, or vice versa—quite the contrary. But this harmony occurs only if it does not imply the otherness of God as manifested solely in relation to Christ. It takes place only in that which has no place, in the reality at once eschatological and utopian which is proper to every creature.

This is precisely what Saint Augustine sets forth with such exceptional power when he writes in his *Confessions:* "Interrogavi terram. . . . Interrogavi mare et abyssos et reptilia animarum vivarum et responderunt: Non sumus Deus tuus. . . . Interrogavi coelum, solem, lunam, stellas: neque nos sumus Deus quem quaeris, inquiunt. Et dixi omnibus his quae circumstant fores carnis meae: dicite mihi de Deo meo, quod vos non estis, dicite mihi de illo aliquid. Et exclamaverunt voce magna: Ipse fecit nos! . . . Et direxi me ad te, et dicite mihi: Tu quis es? Et respondi: Homo!"[12] How restrained this word *homo* sounds in the mouth of the creature par excellence, the very creature God has created in his own image! How restrained it sounds by contrast with all the other creatures who seem to know that they cannot be God only because they "know better." The relationship between creator and creature points to an otherness which in no way can be reduced, were it even by elevating man from nature to spirit.

But let us beware. It is not man caught in the streams of nature, nor is it man atop the highest peaks of the spirit who cries out, *"Homo sum"*; it is man in Christ, the man whose reality is the radical test of the otherness of God, whose past is no longer defined as a source of alienation,[13] and whose future belongs to the unheard-of, the unhoped-for.[14]

From this perspective, and corresponding to creation which endows nature and history not so much with a beginning as with a destiny, we understand the Last Judgment, which does not characterize the end of the world as much as it points out, if

---

12. Saint Augustine, *Confessions,* 10. 6 (Fathers of the Church, Inc., New York, 1953), pp. 270–71: "I asked the earth . . . and the sea, the depths, the creeping things among living animals, and they replied 'We are not thy God, look above us.' . . . I asked the sky, the sun, the moon, the stars: 'Nor are we the God whom you seek,' they said. And I said to all these things which surround the entryways of my flesh: 'Tell me about my God, since you are not He; tell me something about Him.' With a loud voice, they cried out: 'He made us.' . . . Then, I turned to myself and said: 'Who art thou?' And I answered: 'A man.' "
13. John 6:68: "Lord, to whom shall we go? You have the words of eternal life."
14. Rev. 21:5: "Behold, I make all things new."

need be, that God alone can be its end because he is the creator: "It is done! I am the Alpha and the Omega, the beginning and the end. To the thirsty I will give water without price from the fountain of the water of life. He who conquers shall have this heritage, and I will be his God and he shall be my son" (Rev. 21:6–7). It is of this man that the Gospel of John can say: "Truly, truly, I say to you, he who hears my word and believes him who sent me, has eternal life; he does not come into judgment, but has passed from death to life. Truly, truly, I say to you, the hour is coming, and now is, when the dead will hear the voice of the Son of God, and those who hear it will live" (John 5:24–25).

"The hour is coming, and now is. . . ." To the radicalization of the idea of God, and *ipso facto* to the radicalization of the question of man—both achieved by the notion of creation—is quite naturally added the radicalization of all possible finalities effected by the notion of *eschaton*. Moreover, while in the light of creation human nature appears as a technique in which man is no longer trapped in man, a technique which opens up a further promotion of the human, the utopianism implicit in the notion of creation is, in the light of the *eschaton,* manifested neither as end in itself (like some endless speech), nor as closure of man (like some word trapped in its own myth); this utopianism is manifested in a blossoming of the human, here and now, as at the dawn of creation or of the new heaven and the new earth. Terms like son of God, or new man, or even creature, are terms no longer drawn from an idolatrous naturalism. It is by asserting the utopianism conveyed by them that an iconoclastic eschatology asserts its own bearing; it is in their most concrete meaning that, to begin with, such an eschatology acknowledges its own iconoclasm.

Nor is it surprising, therefore, that the naturalism in which, for example, transcendence and immanence become entangled with one another should, without any nostalgia or apprehension, be replaced in such an eschatology by the integral utopianism which is at stake in the fundamental twin notions of *eschaton* and *novum.* While transcendence and immanence have always been more or less fraudulently focused on the idea of a resemblance between God and man, *eschaton* and *novum* are clearly geared to a utopian type of consciousness, according to which

71

between the creator and the creature there can only be, to cite Kierkegaard, an infinite qualitative difference.[15] Moreover, in the first pair the dialectic of resemblance tends to culminate either in a mutual exclusion of God and man or in their reciprocal identification. Only the dialectic of otherness proper to the second pair permits us to avoid these kinds of transpositions, these role reversals, and to check the negation or rejection of utopia that is the eventual result as much of absolutism as of relativism.

To sum up: in depriving itself of the integral utopianism called for by the dialectic of *eschaton* and *novum,* the traditional eschatology of *already* and *not yet*—whether realized or futuristic—makes a gross mistake. Not that this kind of eschatology is espe cially devoid of all utopianism (idealism could easily be one of its more plausible counterfeits); but, profiting illicitly from the radicalization of the idea of God mentioned above, it turns God into a simple absolute.

Is it not, indeed, the same Schleiermacher who, not without good reason, dismisses theism in the name of faith, who just as quickly disguises himself as a most fervent advocate of a monotheism he considers the very essential characteristic of Christianity? Is it not also the immanentist infinitism of Leibniz which turns the idea of God into a kind of absolute, in the light of which necessity is hardly more than an accident and accident hardly less than a necessity?

(2) The New Man, Theater of the Eschaton
In aligning the dialectic of the *eschaton* and the *novum* on a *coincidentia oppositorum* in which transcendence and immanence are the actors *(actants),* soteriological eschatology tends to dissolve the utopianism which funds this dialectic into a simple moment of history; and, at the same time, it shirks the problem of contemporaneity. This problem, as Kierkegaard points out, is the very embodiment of the existential problem. It is the existential problem par excellence. It consists of two levels. In the first place: Do I have any future if everything that I am issues

---

15. Søren Kierkegaard, *The Sickness unto Death* (Princeton University Press, Princeton, 1941).

uniquely from an event which took place two thousand years ago? Second: In what sense is it true that I can have no future except insofar as in Christ I have no past? We draw out the essential thread from the tangled skein of this problem when we ask: Where is the new man? Does he lie upstream or downstream from my own existence? To which we respond: Neither; he lies in Christ. All kinds of implications, and in particular those concerning salvation, immediately flow from this. Salvation does not consist in retrieving the man of today for the benefit of a past religiosity. It consists in the contemporaneity of Christ and the new man. It consists in the advent of man as the human, in man becoming human, the radical condition of God. Such a contemporaneity is precisely what a realized eschatology shirks for the sake of an *already* which occurred, *illic et tunc,* a world ago before my existence *hic et nunc,* here and now. Indeed, if the incarnation, passion, and death of the Son of man serve only to lead man back to Jesus rather than to God, Christ is then nothing more than some leftover Jesus.

In contrast to the realized eschatology which thus succumbs to historicism, futuristic eschatology culminates in apocalypse. Indeed, while for the former the historical alone is eschatological, for the latter the eschatological can only despise the historical. Yet neither the one nor the other brings us to consider the eschatological as the only motive of the historical: that which, precisely, is at stake in all that belongs to history and which, consequently, contributes to the definitions of man in terms of that by which his nature is changed.

We do not, therefore, have to choose between passéism and futurism. The question is not whether the church must be preserved from the world or kept from sinking therein, as a theologian of the caliber of Schillebeeckx fears, while falling back on the comfort provided by a futuristic eschatology.[16] The question is whether the world has a future, and if so, what kind of a future; it is a matter of knowing if the world is to be conceived of as creation, as iconoclasm of everything in nature or in history—in other words, in the status quo—that lays claim to

---

16. "The Interpretation of Eschatology," *Concilium* 41 (Paulist Press, New York, 1969).

hegemony, to autonomy. Such a question can be resolved neither by millenarianism (even one evincing a more or less ecclesiastical character and advocated by a Joachim of Fiore who merely overloads some implications of the thought of Saint Augustine) nor by the politicization of faith (elpidism and Thomism are not as foreign to one another as they might at first seem, particularly to the degree that both demonstrate an equally totalitarian will to synthesize).

If only to give a more concrete aspect to our subject, we recall that traditional eschatology owes its logic to the simple fact that it stifles the utopianism implicit in the notion of the "return of Christ"; it returns us to Jesus rather than leads us to hope in Christ. It makes us search, like the women on the morning of the empty tomb, among the dead for the one who is living (Luke 24:5). "I am the resurrection and the life; he who believes in me, though he die, yet shall he live, and whoever lives and believes in me shall never die" (John 11:25–26; cf. 2 Cor. 4:7–11, 8:15).

Let me summarize:

1. The radicalization of the idea of God that is realized when the Old Testament brings in the notion of the creator and proposes to conceive of God, not as an absolute, but in terms of man, culminates in a questioning of man which is resolved by the corresponding notion of creature. Created in the very image of God, man thus conceives of himself in terms of God, not as an object of manipulation of a nature in which God would in fact have been swallowed up.

2. The utopianism which such a radicalization finally allows to appear is expressive of man's most authentic being. Yet it risks being squandered, unless an equally radical eschatology intervenes to liberate Christology, the doctrine of *man* as revealer of God, and unless at the same time an iconoclastic eschatology liberates Christology from the grip of history.

3. It is only in relation to Christ that the otherness of the creator vis-à-vis the creature, as well as that of the creature vis-à-vis the creator, is upheld. No longer reduced to affirming themselves by excluding one another, God and man occur each one through the other. In order for an iconoclastic eschatology to remain iconoclastic, it must therefore be focused on Christology rather than on theism and, consequently, theodicy. Like

the church, traditional eschatology betrays its triumphalism even when it advocates imitation of the humility of Jesus. From Charybdis to Scylla, it vacillates between a triumphalism that dooms the world to ruin and perdition and an asceticism whose thousand and one sacred hearts of Jesus turn man and his hope away from the utopian face of Christ.

Worse still, in such a perspective the believer is doomed to becoming nostalgic for Jesus rather than freed to live the abundant life of Christ. What is the new man if not the man of the *eschaton,* the man who lies beyond man? What is man in Christ if not the man who, though himself no more than a life spent dying, nevertheless remains futurable: the man who, though he is dead, remains to be lived? Yet, and we know this only too well if the example of the Christian tradition has taught us any kind of lesson, it is by grasping the new man as theater of the *eschaton* that the utopianism proper to the human reality is, for iconoclastic eschatology, lived as radically as possible for man— through faith. But it does not follow that the opposite is equally true; that is, it is not enough for an eschatology to be iconoclastic for it to be certain of avoiding the repudiation of the utopianism it claims to affirm most concretely. As we have tried to show, the dialectic of *already* and *not yet* constitutes, in our opinion, such a repudiation.

As a consequence, it is not enough for an iconoclastic eschatology, in order to sustain its utopianism, to be focused solely on Christology; it must in addition have a trinitarian structure. This condition should not be surprising even after what we said at the beginning of this chapter, for the trinitarian conception of God constitutes the logical fulfillment of the radicalization of the idea of God set forth in the notion of creation, a radicalization to which we owe the affirmation that God is not an absolute but the creator. We must make this affirmation more explicit here by saying: first, it is as articulation of the human reality that God is creator (classical theology expresses this point of view by affirming that it is as father of Jesus Christ that God is creator); and, second, it is as the future of man that God is spirit (classical theology expresses this point of view by saying that it is because God is spirit that man can be his glory and, in Jesus Christ, even be God's condition). In short, the radicalization of the idea of God as set forth by the notion of creation and continued by the trinitarian conception of God does not result in some kind of immanentism. It culminates in an integral utopianism such as can be set in motion by the convergence of the *eschaton* and the *novum* even while, precisely because the human can arise out of all experience of reality, God is the radical "other" though he is present there.

To conclude, it is not only eschatology which assumes a new face when we endow it with a trinitarian schema. The innate utopianism of the human reality also comes into its own, and thereby God is the one who, to speak in classical language, is nearer to man than man is to himself. We will therefore define our position in the following manner.

To the work of the Father corresponds an eschatology of nature, where the polarity of *eschaton* and *novum* appears under the form of creation and vocation; for man is not created in such a way that he can only call upon or recall the reality of God, but also in such a way that he can call it together by means of his own works.

To the work of the Son corresponds an eschatology of history where, in the polarity of incarnation and redemption, destiny is born, not out of an occlusion of history, but from an openness to the future.

To the work of the Spirit—and to the extent that nature and history are thus "desacralized"—corresponds, finally, an eschatology of utopia, that is to say, of the project—including nature and history—of which technique is constitutive, and which is fulfilled by the fact that God is all in all (pleroma) and that man has put on the new man (resurrection).

Though claimed by nature, man can only act as a creature; though claimed by history, he can speak its myth only by assuming his own destiny; though bent on dying, he can imagine living reality only by realizing the experience of his own resurrection: "It is no longer I who live, but Christ who lives in me" (Gal. 2:20).

2. UTOPIA AND TECHNOLOGY

A. The Utopianism of the Real

Despite their brevity, our considerations of the trinitarian structure of eschatology—and consequently of the fundamentally iconoclastic character of all trinitarian eschatology—allow us to develop the threefold attribution which qualifies the *eschaton,* namely, first as principle of creation, then as principle of destination, and, finally, as principle of novation.

(1) Ethics and Iconoclasm
As a matter of fact, by thus isolating these three principles, we are doing nothing less than establishing the basis for an ethic of the kingdom. We do so not out of nostalgia for a triumphalist and now outdated vocabulary, but simply because, *volens nolens,* we must still cope with the components of such an ethic. These components are (1) the iconoclastic notion of vocation, and its corollary the idea of social mobility in view of the equality of all men before the human; in comparison, traditional theology does not dare to advocate more than a distributive regime of stability which found its balance, if not in the status quo, at least in the maintenance of statutes based on the simple fact of being born as so-and-so; (2) the equally iconoclastic notion of the responsibility of the believer for the nonbeliever, of the Christian for the non-Christian; for, in Christ, there is neither Jew nor Greek, neither male nor female; and, as a consequence, it is less the church than the world which is the instrument of the grace of God; in comparison, traditional theology subdues the responsibility of the believer and submits it to the messianism of the *extra ecclesiam nulla salus;* and (3) the no less iconoclastic notion of freedom: not the freedom which sees itself as paroled in the world as long as the hold of the flesh endures (for traditional theology easily falls into the error of seeing in the dualistic conception of a supernatural world the utopian expression of the human reality), but the glorious liberty of the *children* of

God (Rom. 8:21); not the alienating freedom which nonetheless still makes man a product of nature or of history, but the freedom which through Christ makes him a co-worker with God (1 Cor. 3:8), the very condition of God (as attested to by the genealogies which, to speak traditionally, define Jesus as "the son of Adam, the son of God"; cf. Luke 3:23–38).

This point is obvious: we are far from—indeed at the other extreme from—the *Interimsethik* advocated by Albert Schweitzer, who wrote, perhaps unawares, that "the kingdom of God is super-moral,"[17] the ultimate expression of an idealism by definition unrealizable from the point of view of our supposedly more human conceptions of ethics. Schweitzer, unfortunately, was consistent with himself, but only at the price of betraying his own intuitions, only by seeing in the ethic of Jesus the unequaled expression of an absolute idealism rather than the most straightforward requirement for a most utopian iconoclasm. It was Schweitzer himself who wrote: "Every ethical norm of Jesus, be it ever so perfect, leads therefore only up to the frontier of the Kingdom of God, while every trace of a path disappears so soon as one advances upon the new territory. There one needs it no more."[18] And for a very good reason! In Jesus' understanding, the ethic of the kingdom is not explained through some sort of wait-and-see attitude, but through its iconoclasm; it does not wait to blossom forth when a propitious environment turns up, but on the contrary upsets all ideas that man has of his own worth. For the kingdom of God in no way resembles the kingdoms of this world. And yet this is precisely the reason why the eschatological code of the kingdom is eminently pertinent to this world, in that it is realizable if only the world consents to be challenged, *hic et nunc,* without waiting for some kind of preliminary conditioning. Jesus himself expresses this when he says, for example, "The kingdom of God is *as if* a man should scatter seed upon the ground . . ."; or again, "With what can we compare the kingdom of God, or what parable shall we use for it? It is *like* a mustard seed . . ." (Mark 4:26,

---

17. Albert Schweitzer, *The Mystery of the Kingdom of God* (A. & C. Black, London, 1925), p. 102.
18. Ibid., p. 102.

30–31). Idealism? No indeed! Rather, it is a utopianism, one all the more radical because it imprints, not an ethic of the unrealizable, that is to say in the final analysis, an ethic of compromise, but exactly an ethic of the realizable, in the light of which the same can be said of the things of God *as* of those of men, and of God *as* of man.

We can order the components of an ethic of the kingdom as follows: considered as principle of creation, the *eschaton* appears as constitutive of nature; considered as redemption or destiny, the *eschaton* appears as constitutive of history; considered as pleroma, the *eschaton* appears, finally, as constitutive of utopia. In such a schema nature, history, and utopia must not be considered as phases succeeding one another; all three are implied in one another since each one equally well represents a particular exigency of the technique they hold in common, that of the human. This technique of the human is exactly what is in question when notions such as creation, destiny, or pleroma arise. We can therefore say that if creation constitutes the *novum* of nature, and destiny that of history, it is in the pleroma that we must situate the *novum* of utopia. But we should no more consider nature, history, and utopia as so many realms, epochs, or ages that man successively crosses, than we should see in creation, destiny, and pleroma the stages of some evolutionistic view of man's salvation. For the God who reigns is the one who saves, as he is also the God who creates.

(2) The Kingdom of Man and Its Powers
Nature, history, and utopia constitute, so to speak, the various powers of the kingdom of man: a kingdom which, because it is completely focused on the *novum,* on the impossible possibility of reducing the human to man, serves mainly to show that in spite of appearances the promotion of the human is not to be confused with the "return to nature"; that it is in spite of history that man can, in reality, assume his destiny; that thanks to utopia it is not possible to reduce nature to naturalism or history to historicism. Man indeed transcends man, and we should no more reduce humanity to the level of "hominity" than we should reduce God to the ranks of the divinities, the adoration of which leads man both to attain his integrity and to disin-

tegrate. Nature, history, and utopia are, each in its own way, factors favoring the emancipation of man; on the other hand, it is no less true that man is man only if he is emancipated from these very factors, only if he is considered as creature, that is to say, as new man.

To be sure, as new man, man continues to belong to nature, but only to the extent that, echoing it, he distinguishes himself from it and transcends it. He continues to belong to history but only to the extent that, receiving it as an inheritance, he can carve a destiny out of it. Geared to utopia, man is above all, among the living, the one limited neither by birth nor by death. As Geertz points out, while each man has a birthday, man as such does not.[19] Mythologically speaking, he has no father but a Father; he is not engendered but created; he is a creature, or, in other words, man come of age, and not that phony orphan of God we have heard about over and over again since Bonhoeffer.[20]

Contrary to prevailing notions, religion does not mark an infantile stage in the development of man; rather, it indicates the utopian thrust of the process of humanization. And from this perspective, it is less the liberation of man that we should see in the "death of the Father" than the impossibility of a return to childhood, or rather a return to nature. The "death of the Father" represents, if we can put it this way, the expression par excellence of anti-utopianism. At the very least, it is the expression of the fundamental ambiguity which lies in the heart of man and which, under the pretext of emancipation, tends in fact to withdraw man from the human, or which, under the pretext of returning man to nature, robs him of his true project, the project by which, as he discloses himself as "revealer" of God, man is by reason of his creatureliness called to be the very condition of God. Is this not, moreover, the reason why the whole Christian tradition has always refused to assimilate the

---

19. Clifford Geertz, "The Impact of the Concept of Culture on the Concept of Man," in *New Views of the Nature of Man,* ed. J. Platt (University of Chicago Press, Chicago, 1965); cf. Edgar Morin, *Le paradigme perdu: la nature humaine* (Editions du Seuil, Paris, 1973), p. 63.
20. Dietrich Bonhoeffer, *Letters and Papers from Prison* (New York, Macmillan, 1972).

death of Christ to some kind of "death of the Father," proclaiming instead that with the coming of Christ it is the Father who is given to us? To be sure, we already knew this: like all the parables, that of the prodigal son is determined above all by its eschatological orientation. All the same, it receives an even better reading when we let it show that even if the process of hominization is *per se* irreversible, it is not enough to tip man into the human, to switch him from childhood to adulthood, from nature to maturity. Needed, here, is another process, that of humanization. But at this point—which hominization left to itself could not attain—through an interplay of language proper to man, the reality of God, far from being imposed from on high, enters or bursts forth in the human reality. And both God and man embody one another.

At this point, God is no longer even "necessary," as classical theology would contend, knowing all the while that it was driven to such formulations through the logic of its system much more than because they complied with its own understanding of faith. As we say today, correcting tendencies that classical theology itself would have unhesitatingly repudiated, God is no stopgap such that he would only serve to fill loopholes haphazardly opened by random mutations of nature. He is radically other as much in relation to nature as in relation to man. By the same token, he is the one whose reality emerges only through humanization, but in such a way that, on the one hand, this reality of God cannot possibly be excluded from this process without man denying himself and that, on the other hand, at each point of this process a point of no return is reached. We are led, then, to the following affirmation: in the same way as we can say that it is language which has created man, and not the other way around,[21] we can also say first that it is humanization which has rendered hominization possible as well as realizable, and second that it is God who has created man and not man God. Surely, for such an affirmation not to lose its foothold, we must add that only the living are capable of praising God (Isa. 38:19), and that this God—the God of Abraham, the God of Isaac and the God of Jacob—is not the God of the dead but of the living

---

21. Morin, p. 87.

(Matt. 22:32; Mark 12:27; Luke 20:38). Therefore what characterizes the reign of man is that he does not become encysted like a monolith in his own totality. What characterizes him most profoundly is, instead, his openness; and the most radical openness with which he can be and is endowed is certainly the openness which leads to God.

(3) Humanization and the Quest of the Novum

Nature, history, and utopia are three stances of the same tropism, all governed by the quest for the *novum*. Each of them, though it expresses the human reality, nevertheless lacks what we have called the *eschaton*. In the *eschaton* we must now find the very root of hope that, in one leap, switches man from the animal to the human, from nature to creature, from history to destiny, and from totalitarian universalism to the pleroma. In this respect, the *eschaton* is both what we believe in when we see the spectacle of the reality of God in the world, and what we can see of the spectacle of the world when we believe in the reality of God; it molds man's hope even though man has been everywhere and seen everything that is to be seen of the kingdom of man—like Jesus, who at the time of the temptation in the desert (Matt. 4:1; Mark 1:12; Luke 4:1) somehow finds himself hoisted up to the pinnacle of hominization and shows that the human cannot grow or the animal diminish there (John 3:30) unless the glory of God sounds through the glory of man. For the living, who alone can praise God, only live through symbiosis with God. This is how man inhabits man and how the human face of heaven, the gaze of God, can shine on earth (Num. 6:25; Ps. 67:2).

One thing must be clear: we are not trying to retrieve the old dichotomy of the natural and the supernatural, a dichotomy by virtue of which the reign of God consisted in colonizing the reign of man if not in merely annexing it. We advocate no such *Anschluss* in the name of a kingdom of God disseminated throughout the world. Our goal is not to be confused with the aims of a triumphalistic apologetic. Nor does it consist in a surreptitious elaboration of an apologetic of the catacombs. The imperialism with which Christian faith could be rigged is alien to us but we also refuse to let ourselves be overcome by the wave—or the fad—of "miserabilism" which seems prevalent today.

In appealing to the notion of God, we are only trying to speak better of man, to discern in man the hope of the human. It is not possible to say it without malice: the more we know about the process of hominization, the less we know about man. Let science do what it may to disclose the genesis of man, he remains a mystery to us, at least so long as language endures, stretching him between the imaginary and the real, between God and the beast. In order for God to exist, man must hope and be able to speak. Through language, God bursts forth in the human reality: indeed, has the incarnation of the Word ever meant anything else? Man is the event of God. If it is important for man to know the date of his birth, he will not truly know its meaning unless he undergoes a new birth. Without *novitas,* man would only have come into the world stillborn. But without *eschaton,* it is impossible to speak of a new birth.

Thus we are neither astonished nor shocked that after having described how *"homo sapiens* carries the possibility, the genetic and cerebral promise of a supercomplex society which has yet to see the light of day but whose need is felt," and after having said why we can, with this understanding, "foresee, hope, and call for a fourth birth of humanity,"[22] Edgar Morin completes the critique he levels at man, dehumanized during so many centuries of hominism, by concluding that we need a new *scienza nuova,* a new utopianism of language which would unfurl over the whole reign of man. Perhaps a new metaphysics will come which will allow us to fill "the tremendous chasm which is widening between science and values,"[23] the intolerable chasm which grows as science chooses to occupy itself with mere bureaucratic imperatives and to delay the maturation of a knowledge of man finally consonant with genuine scientific knowledge. Idolatry and ideology go hand in hand. Together they constitute the epicenter of this counter-utopia which consists in attempting the impossible, the unlikely return to nature, and, like the children of Israel before the golden calf during the

---

22. Ibid., p. 209.
23. Ibid., p. 230.

Exodus, refusing the inevitable, the only thing realizable, the Promised Land (Exod. 32).

In the same way that man is the event of God, utopia is the event of the kingdom, and *novum* the event of the *eschaton*. For all this, God is not conceived as more necessary to man than is humanization (in an understanding of man stripped of all anthropologism and all biologism) in relation to hominization. Rather, we thereby recover our previous claim about the biblical notion of creation and about the eschatological iconoclasm—in the strongest sense of that term—of all hominism as well as of all deism. And if the believer can say that what God has joined together must not be separated, it behooves the unbeliever—who is natural man, the man of nature—to refrain from separating what life, with its utopian drive, has likewise joined together —God and man. Nor could we, under these conditions, accuse the believer of deserting man simply because he then confesses that this union is realized through the word made flesh, through this utopian metaphor of the *novitas,* the Christ, Son of man, Son of God.

B. Technological Utopianism

I will limit myself to a few points that have no other aim than to locate technological utopianism in relation to the various topographies of utopia in general, as experienced all along the adventure of human consciousness.

From this perspective, let us begin by pointing out that for some utopia lies beyond culture, while others place it within. Sometimes utopia is confused with the land of milk and honey, sometimes with the millennium. Furthermore, some are prone to imagining its prime motive as an irrepressible nostalgia for nature, or else as a no less irrepressible revenge of history. We have also seen how[24] Some can define utopia in opposition to ideology while others—Christians, obviously—are tempted to oppose it to the kingdom of God as if it could only be the latter's counterfeit.

---

24. Cf. Chapter II.

However, without obstinately persisting in disparaging history and nature, we have shown that ideology, bridled by history, distorts utopia, while metaphysics, trapped as it is in nature, leads it astray. Considered as a technique of human techniques, utopia is rather tied to what one could call a meta-technique. The difference between such a meta-technique on the one hand and metaphysics or its ideological counterpart on the other is of major importance. Indeed, there is a clear line of demarcation between the two. On one side, man is still understood either in terms of a specific human nature or as a kind of iceberg whose visible part would only be the playoff of the part hidden *in* or *by* nature. On the other side, the forces at work unleashing the very possibility of any process of humanization stem much less from nature than from art; they stem from *techne,* from technique or even from artifice itself. It is by a similar approach that Ernst Bloch is led to assert the emergence of hope as the dividing line between a form of utopia henceforth dominated by the idea of the *novum* and all those which precede it.[25] The latter pivot around that which is possible because it is necessary, inasmuch as it harks back either to nature or to history. But only the realizable, which calls upon the imaginary, is capable of emancipating man from both, thereby bringing hope within reach.

(1) Art and Technè: The Human as Artifice

Like history, nature in itself has no other goal than to restrain utopia.[26] Of course, to the extent that hominization consists in the vertical position of man, it facilitates access to a higher level of humanization. But this does not automatically have the effect of rendering man, who considers himself civilized, any less cruel than the barbarian. At the very least, he is partial to a somewhat more refined cruelty. To the extent that man has had to renounce or overcome this cruelty, it is obvious that he has done and can do so only through artifice, the twofold artifice posing as myth of man or as technique of the human. But while from

---

25. Cf. Bloch, *Man on His Own,* pp. 82, 83, 121, 126.
26. Cf. Seiji Nutia, "Traditional Utopias in Japan and the West," in *Aware of Utopia,* ed. David Plath (University of Illinois Press, Urbana, 1971), p. 18.

one stage of the human to the other the rise of man perhaps conceals his cruelty, it never conceals his artificiality. Indeed, were man to elevate himself to the point of taking himself for a god, he would not have become a man.

Artifice remains no less a quality of which all myths of man avail themselves and by which all technique of the human ennobles itself. In support of such an affirmation, it is enough to consider in the same light what happens to another pairing whose terms we like to set in opposition today: nature and culture. Quite willing to associate myth and nature on the one hand, and technology and culture on the other, a certain contemporary fad consists of denouncing culture by accusing it of being alienating, while at the same time unjustly accusing technology of despoiling nature by destroying its myth. Yet if it is true that technology and culture go together, nothing is less certain than the linking of myth to nature. The closer we look, the more we perceive what the true role of myth has been. Myth has not brought man back to nature so much as it has sought to settle him in culture. Indeed, myth has consisted primarily in a quest for harmony between man and his culture. In contrast, all technology insofar as it concerns the human, and thus insofar as it means becoming conscious of nature, aims essentially at harmonizing man with nature.

Even if today we must in some respects contrast mythology and technology, the fact remains that myth and technique, the mythique of man and the technique of the human, have always coexisted. At the very least, the mythique of man has always included a technique of the human. The difference is that at one point the process of humanization seems to be the effect of some pressure from below, at another of some thrust from above. In the first case, man adapts himself to the world but not without adopting it; in the second, he adopts the world but not without adapting to it. From this follow two points which need to be stressed.

1. In spite of appearances, myth, readily considered natural, in fact challenges nature—either because the latter is hostile to man or because it determines him—even if this challenge takes the unfortunate shape of a flight from the world into apocalypse. But this is not surprising: being fundamentally anamnes-

tic in its very structure, myth ultimately confuses the *novum* with the *initium*. As for apocalypse, what is it if not the utter negation of all that separates man from his origins? Nor should we forget that in this respect all classical utopias since Plato are either idealistic or perfectionistic, and that they are unrealizable simply because in them nature, like paradise, is experienced only as something lost.

2. Likewise, and this once again in spite of appearances, we must stress that the technique of the human, even though it is readily considered anti-naturalistic, is by its very essence threatened by naturalism—as is clear from all the allegations that it is dehumanizing or depersonalizing. In contrast to myth, for which apocalypse constitutes the supreme temptation, technology is tormented by a temptation which wears the mask of a newfangled ideology, namely technocracy, a sort of earthly paradise which no less than the lost paradise negates man. Where myth, allegedly concerned with nature alone, in fact ends up with apocalypse, technology, relentlessly charged with apocalypse (in every sense of the term), in fact constantly collides with that which we continue to call human nature and which (because we fail to live up to it) we sometimes tend to pursue in the counter-utopia of what Foucault calls the "rêverie of the beginnings."[27]

(2) Humanization and Incarnation

What was said of nature and grace in medieval thought can also be said of myth and technique. Technique—or for that matter technology—does not abolish myth but fulfills it. In distinguishing them, we have simply sought to show how the Christian faith can invest the substantial resources already stored in the nascent technological civilization. The elucidation of faith requires a similar clarification of the human phenomenon as it is affected by a technological civilization, and as it henceforth takes on a dynamic rather than a static character.

However, our inquiry has also shown that whatever the scheme, man generally stands under the same vantage point X

27. Michel Foucault, *Les Mots et les choses* (Gallimard, Paris 1966), p. 274; *The Order of Things* (Random House, New York, 1973).

(utopia). Depending on the circumstances, A (nature) and B (history), at least at first glance, seem for various reasons as different from one another as from C (technology) in particular. One must not, however, exclude the possibility that A, B, and C are only variants of a constant identical project and that they are, if not indebted to one another, at least linked together if only one could view them under angle Y (eschatology). One must not exclude the possibility that nature, history, and technology are elements of a single design, and that they constitute, each in its own way, as many techniques of the human as correspond to their respective utopianisms.

But even if coordinated in this way with their respective utopianisms, these techniques culminate either in a flight into the past (rêverie of the beginnings) or in a flight forward (apocalyptic futurism) or even[28] in a flight within (Dionysiac liberation of the body instead of the soul). The result is that the utopian reality proper to man himself is short-circuited, and an intolerable gap is felt between utopia and the real. The task is thus to give utopia—technological or otherwise—its character as eschatological code, much as we are able to consider the human reality as a code of the divine when it discloses itself as the very event of God. What are humanization and incarnation, if not the two sides of one and the same reality from which God emerges as the radically other so long as man remains to be realized?

Except where the biblical theme of the incarnation is concerned, mythological utopianism is idealistic and perfectionistic, as is, on the whole, the ideological messianism which determines the utopianism of history. In contrast to both, technological utopianism is above all pragmatic; and it is pluralistic, even if coercive metamorphoses can be sensed, owing to the residual ideologies which defraud the possibilities of technology.

Anyhow, in the schema we are outlining, mythological utopianism corresponds to A (nature), ideological utopianism to B (history), and, finally, technological utopianism to C (technique). Moreover, if X (utopia) finds its referent in the process of humanization, incarnation belongs to eschatology (Y). Thus

---

28. Cf. below, Chapter V, sections 2 and 3 in particular.

God and man form a dyad, the only one which constantly reflects, through its various homeostases, the unique reality from which God can emerge as the radically other and man can still realize himself.

These homeostases display characteristics which at one moment bring them close to one another and at another moment separate them from one another.

Able to affect both mythological utopianism (for example, in the techniques of the sacred) and technological utopianism (for example, in technocracy), ideology thus appears as an intermediary form between myth and technology.

Myth is anthropocentric; technology is not. As for ideology, it errs in not being anthropocentric from the vantage point of mythology, while it errs in being anthropocentric from the vantage point of technology. More particularly, myth exhausts itself in anthropologism but redeems itself by addressing the question of God to man. Technology exhausts itself in biologism, but redeems itself by addressing man to the question of God, establishing it on an order other than that of nature or history, namely on the order of the living. From the anthropological to the biological, then from the biological to the living, these are the three successive phases of the contract of humanization between God, the radically other, on the one hand, and man, who must not be confused with the human, on the other. Nature, history, and technology have in turn honored this oft-challenged but never-canceled contract. The remarks which follow, and the threefold reflection which they entail, are based on this contention.

First, as long as technology is confined strictly to the periphery of the human order, man never experiences it as a threat—on the contrary. It is only from the moment that it penetrates the human order and interferes with its trajectory that technology becomes threatening, even hostile. In opposition to myth, which comforts the human order and interiorizes it to the extent of shrinking man to his inner self, technology disturbs this order and challenges man. By exteriorizing man, technology immediately opens man to that which lies beyond man, to the human, to the very life which myth always depicts as a future life.

Second, technological utopianism implies not only that man leave nature behind but also that he abandon history.[29] Man does not install himself in the human, he anticipates it. Humanization, then, does not consist in realizing some sort of utopia; rather, it is utopia which consists in the realization of the man who anticipates the human. To be sure, as Teilhard de Chardin has pointed out, it is only in hindsight that we become aware of the mutations which take place in the human order. Man, Pascal would have said, would know neither how to believe nor how to hope in God unless his heart were sensitive to God after the event, or, rather, beforehand. For to whom could we liken God, or what image could we contrive of him (Isa. 40:18)? And who is Christ if not the man beforehand? Or what is the risen Christ if not Jesus and therefore, a fortiori, man after the event, man whom God has brought out of Egypt, the world of counter-utopia par excellence?

Ernst Bloch himself points out that when the believer, the new man, is exhorted not to conform to this world, it is to the world of counter-utopia that the New Testament refers.[30] But we should only leave the world as we leave Egypt, and it is in an analogous way that we should leave nature behind and let history bury its dead; it is in an analogous way, also, that the two are to be desacralized if indeed the world is to become an arena for the reign of God, the theater of his glory. It is said that technology desacralizes. But neither faith nor technology regards the sacred as the only viable form of transcendence. There is also utopia, or the Promised Land, or the reign of God —all things which, above all else, must not be sacralized, and which, like all utopias, are by definition desacralizing.[31] Not that man must be removed from the sacred. Rather, what must be recovered is the utopian dimension underlying the sacred, and which is therefore proper to man. Nor does the Bible affirm

---

29. Cf. Emmanuel Mesthene, "Technology and Humanistic Values," in *Technology, Human Values and Leisure,* ed. Max Kaplan and Phillip Bosserman (Abingdon Press, Nashville, 1971), p. 53; Morin, p. 207; on another level of ideas whose preoccupations nonetheless meet ours, cf. likewise Barth, *Church Dogmatics,* I/2, sec. 20, 1, p. 546.
30. In *Man on His Own.*
31. What a contrast there is between the faith of Saint Thomas More the martyr and the "religion" of his *Utopia!* Cf. Jean Servier, *Histoire de l'Utopie* (Gallimard, Paris, 1967).

anything else when it declares that all holiness belongs to God alone, to the *eschaton*.

Third, since technology appears today as the sole vector of this utopianism, the world once again runs the risk of becoming unlivable[32]—for lack of a utopia. Nor is it just a question of utilizing technology or taking advantage of its multiple applications. For this, nothing more than a cultural revolution would be required. But, as Malraux puts it, in order for man still to use his soul, still to serve others, he will have to undergo nothing less than conversion.[33]

In order to "find" God, we must be able to seek man. We must seek man wherever he can be found, in his random mutations and through whatever techniques of the human, or even in spite of them. The human cannot be reduced to mere technique. And the technological civilization which will have survived its cultural revolution will have to learn this above all, precisely because such a civilization will have ceased to be anthropocentric.

The one thing we must not lose sight of at any cost is that humanization cannot be derived from technology, any more than it has, until now, been automatically raised from the effects of hominization. If man shows goodness, is it not very often due to the fact that he cannot behave otherwise, and that, far from obliterating human responsibility, this commits him to it even more freely?

If we admit that technological utopianism is not anthropocentric, it does not follow that man is ruled out. Nor is it in the least excluded that technology confronts man with the human, involving him in a new adventure of that otherness of God of which the human body is the instrument, the event, the incarnation.

---

32. Cf. John R. Platt: "The World has become too dangerous for anything less than utopia" (quoted by Buckminster Fuller, *Utopia or Oblivion* [Bantam, New York, 1969], p. 288); René Dumont, *L'Utopie ou la mort* (Editions du Seuil, Paris, 1973).
33. Cf. Gabriel Vahanian, "Beyond the Death of God: The Need of a Cultural Revolution," Dialog I (1962):4, and *Wait Without Idols* (Braziller, New York, 1964).

V

Ecclesial Revolution
and Technological Society

1. ECCLESIAL REVOLUTION AND THE UTOPIANISM OF THE HUMAN REALITY

If the preceding chapter concluded by showing that a cultural revolution was inconceivable without a "conversion" of man, we must now begin by affirming the converse: changing man without changing life would be a luxury which only spoiled children in search of exotica could for a while indulge with impunity.

In terms of classical theology, it is not salvation which inaugurates the kingdom of God, but the coming of the kingdom which makes the proclamation of salvation possible. For faith consists not in displacing but in transcending religion. And Christianity accordingly is not a mystery religion of salvation. Inasmuch as it calls for transcending all religion, Christianity is the vector of every utopian anticipation of the kingdom. At the base of Christianity there is, not Jesus who brought salvation because he would be the Christ, but Jesus who is the Christ because he brings salvation. And salvation is not to be gained by fleeing the world, but by changing life in the act of changing the world.

This means that faith in Christ (the conversion of man) would have amounted merely to the pursuit of an empty chimera if at the same time there had not occurred a true cultural revolution, that is, an ecclesial revolution: the deaf hear, the blind see, the lame walk, and, moreover, all form one body since in Christ "there is neither Jew nor Greek, neither slave nor freedman, neither male nor female" (Gal. 3:28).

I would argue that this means that whatever the origins of technology, it is in the church, namely, the church as the political and social dimension of faith as well as its cultural iconoclasm,[1] that technological society takes root. The ecclesial reality of faith, understood as eschatological principle of political and social organization of the human order, is what renders possible the emergence of a technological society by preparing its access to the human order: an order still reflected in the givens of nature with its separation of men and women, or in the facts of history with its discrimination of Jews and Greeks, rather than in the technological phenomenon of the human, the technological understanding of man.

Not that without Christianity technology would not have seen the light of day—in certain respects, that is something not totally inconceivable. But, without the utopianism of the ecclesial revolution begun almost two thousand years ago (though still no more than "begun"), the fundamental options characteristic of technological society would all have escaped the control of utopia and would have belonged instead to some sort of nirvana. The proof of this is the attraction that the religions of the Far East exert today on post-Christian man, at once marginally Western and Christianity's orphan. Now then, in the wake of the ecclesial revolution, how could it be that technology, which threatens contemporary secular ideologies as well as the religious residues accompanying them, can challenge this utopianism? How could technology possibly disavow the utopianism of a church which, historically speaking, sees the light of day when the ethnocentric messianism of Israel and the anthropocentric naturalism of the Roman Empire both collapse at one stroke; a messianism and a naturalism of which the church will, nevertheless, be careful enough not to disavow either the utopianism or the humanism? The ecclesial revolution begins with a revolution of the human phenomenon. What a shock! For the Greeks

---

1. Obviously such a description does not apply to a church cut off from this dimension and rendered inert, hampered by its own institutions.

who do not believe what they hear and for the Jews who do not believe what they see, the church constitutes the real "future shock."

But whether Jew or Greek, every man is able to devalue faith by transforming it into religiosity, or to turn utopia into apocalypse. Every man is capable on his own of denying man. And it is the ensuing depersonalizing conception of man and dehumanization of society that Jesus denounces when he attacks those who want a sign from heaven, but are incapable of believing their own eyes. Jesus tells them: "The sabbath was made for man, not man for the sabbath; so the Son of man is lord even of the sabbath" (Mark 2:27–28). Likewise, to the adherents of the law (whether *torah* or *lex* or *nomos* in general, it does not matter),[2] Saint Paul has no difficulty pointing out that without a continual reconversion of man, without a permanent conversion, there would no more be any sort of humanization than there would be a sanctification of the sabbath or the kingdom. He writes: ". . . I do not do what I want, but I do the very thing I hate. . . . For I delight in the law of God in my inmost self, but I see in my members another law at war with the law of my mind and making me captive to the law of sin which dwells in my members" (Rom. 7:15, 22–23).

Unlike the soteriological religiosity of myth, focused on the return of man to his origins, the church, the eschatic body of Christ, takes place only where it can valorize the utopian dimension of the human reality. It thus proclaims that the utopianism of the human reality is vindicated less through apocalypticism than through rebirth (1 Pet. 1:3), less through the knowledge of facts than through the knowledge of faith (1 Cor. 13:2, 9). The apostle Paul casts it in a striking way: "For Jews demand signs and Greeks seek wisdom, but we preach Christ crucified, a stumbling block to Jews and folly to the Gentiles, but to those who are called, both Jews and Greeks, Christ is the power of God and the wisdom of God" (1 Cor. 1:22–23).

What exactly is this thing that is a stumbling block for some and folly for others? Nothing less than the vindication of man,

---

2. Cf. Franz-J. Leenhardt, *L'Epitre de saint Paul aux Romains* (Delachaux et Niestlé, Neuchâtel/Paris, 1957), p. 102.

which both Jews and Greeks accuse the ecclesial revolution of advocating in the name of a *technique*[3] of the human that strikes at the root of all preconceived notions about man. What is the reason for this accusation? It is that the believer affirms that man, once out of his mother's womb, is no longer limited by birth or by death, but by flesh and spirit, by Adam and the Christ, the *novum* and the *eschaton,* utopia and the kingdom: he has sided with life and can, as a consequence, be numbered among those who alone can praise God. As the permanence of a radical cultural revolution (which is not satisfied with changing society but aims as well at liberating man from any determinism that impedes reconversion to the human or integration of man's own reality), the church is contemporary with the world if the God it proclaims is a God who comes into the world, and if reciprocally the world is event of the kingdom.

And that we are dealing with utopia only where we are dealing with the realizable is, moreover, what the church affirms when, discerning in man the very condition of God, it affirms that the eschatological alone is historical (1 Cor. 15:12–21). So that man, geared to utopia even though stemming from nature or bound to history, far from being eliminated, is then inaugurated; prolepsis of man, he participates in the liturgy of the world and celebrates the advent of God. Besides, how could man, matrix of the technique of the human, consist in anything else?

But it is not enough for man merely to be an extension of man, so to speak; he must also be changed. Wanderer and vagabond, man escapes man. A fugitive before God, he can only take refuge in the human where God awaits him. Not, however, as in those emanationist theories of antiquity where man was merely held on a leash, bound as he was to an origin of origins. But rather, projected ahead of himself and disposing of no more than himself, he must improvise (as he does when he assumes his own destiny) the supreme contingency which consists in defeating all the determinisms that pretend to be the bearers of meaning.

---

3. There is no other term either for the Jews imbued with last ends or for the Greeks imbued with first beginnings.

Thus, in developing natural man with a view toward a nature proper to the human, man can assume nature itself; he no longer needs to domesticate it. Nor does he need to abdicate before history when he assumes what we must continue to call destiny (in spite of the bad usage to which the term is subjected). Is it not in a similar order of ideas that, contrary to his contemporaries who locked Israel in its history, Jesus for his part sees only the occasion to invite all men to assume destiny as they would contingency?

In the light of these observations, our point is thus confirmed: namely, that man is and always has been technological man, if only because technique exists from the moment that man invents himself, realizes himself. By thus acknowledging "man as a technique" we designate every process of humanization undertaken in the name of a utopianism which nothing given beforehand, whether sacred or profane, can wholly satisfy, and which, for this reason, is sometimes realized through an apparent permutation of the sacred and the profane. Thus, when one speaks of "human nature," the fact is that nature considered as a personification of the gods has already been desacralized; and history itself is on the verge of so becoming when man comes to grasp himself as freedom.[4]

We can now better define this utopianism of the human reality by stating that it consists in the "new man" who transcends the dialectic of man and the human, of hominization and humanization, and, likewise, of flesh and spirit, of art and artifice. It assumes the form of a technique set in motion by the necessity of making a clean sweep of everything in man which appears to be only a residue of the human. For the human is man without prototype, and man consists solely in being formed by that which he neither has nor is. To be sure, we have been accustomed to "believe" that Adam was the first man—at the cost, however, of turning faith into an ideology. But the notion of creation has never meant that such a man was the prototype of all others. Instead, the very thing which makes Adam a "son of

---

4. It can be noted in passing that on this point Saint Augustine is neither a metaphysician (as we usually imagine), nor even the first theologian of history, but a radical utopian.

God" is the type, likewise, of all creatures. Real humanization does not even deal with any descent from Adam; it is concerned only with sonship in relation to God. Even in the Gospel, Adam is not the prototype of Jesus—first born from among the dead, the new Adam—by reason of a lineage according to the flesh, but by reason of his being "son of God": a creature, namely, that which allows for Jesus himself to be the condition of Christ.[5] In addition, true humanization is an eschatological adventure, an adventure of God's bodying forth into the human. The man who dwells in man inaugurates the advent of God, the articulation of man by the human, outside of which every dialectic of body and soul, of flesh and spirit, identity and difference, is doomed to failure.

Embodying that which is other, even that which is radically other, man bodies forth into himself. Hence, it is not "I" who am an other; instead, through this embodiment of man as the locus of his own integration, it is man in his entirety who is other. Man, then, is something other than an unbridling of man in the body, something other than a dionysiac disembodiment or a dislocation of the body and the soul, a mystique of the soul, a disincarnate spirituality. As a matter of fact, the utopianism of the human reality could even, in the final analysis, consist of the Promethean concatenation of man by man, if not quite the vertiginous concelebration of the human, rather than of any dionysiac disembodiment of it. Rather than resacralizing residues of man by way of a life lived only for the body or only for the soul, it is time for that soul to depart, and for the body, ceasing to be expelled, to recover its proper vocation as temple of the spirit, which consists in witnessing to the humanity of God, to the human as co-humanity. Indeed, it is through the body that the utopianism constitutive of the human reality makes itself felt and is realized, through a body which, like an empty tomb, is the first fruit of the resurrection and its prolepsis rather than, as Saint Paul says, "the body of this death" (Rom. 7:24), the body where death holds us sequestered.

Sluice of being, the utopianism of the human reality is what holds in check every disconnection that would attenuate man;

---

5. According to Luke, the so-called historian among the evangelists; cf. 3:23–38.

flaming tongue loosening the human reality, it defuses the apocalyptics of the body and catalyzes the human in terms of technique, regardless of the latter's norm, nature, history, or technology; a technique of the human which, by necessity, is at once
desacralizing and sacralizing, liberating and alienating, if only
because it is neither gnosis, nor anamnesis, nor, above all, a
program. Moreover, this explains why, notwithstanding the intrinsic neutrality of human techniques, their emergence coin-
cides with a displacement of the sacred. Sacred history thus
replaces the divine conception of nature. Similarly, we must
acknowledge that if technology has been a factor of desacralization it has also been, by compensation, a factor of sacralization[6]
at least with respect to the body, mediator between man and the
human.

Yet, this is still not the issue. It is in fact possible that in
moving from mythology to technology, we only shift from one
system of the sacred to another. But, no less certainly, we shift
from a civilization of the soul to a civilization of the body.

Technological civilization is, indeed, a civilization of the
body. Bringing man down to earth, it gives him back an earthly
dimension heretofore neglected in favor of the soul and its
heavenly aspirations. And, by the same token, the church also
discovers its last chance—or should; long dedicated to guaranteeing individual salvation, it is finally available to gather all
men into the body of Christ.

Totalitarianism or pleroma—what will be the fundamental
choice of the technological civilization?

In response to those who see it leaning toward totalitarianism
because of the automatism through which they view all technique, we can bring two objections to bear.

On the one hand, we must ask whether the notion of automatism does not really draw its inspiration from the more or less
mechanistic conception of the "laws of nature" which the fraud-
ulent modern epoch has substituted for the ancient "natural
law," more than it is inspired by the mechanistic tendencies
unjustly attributed to the technological phenomenon.[7]

---

6. Cf. Jacques Ellul, *The New Demons* (Seabury Press, New York, 1975), p. 75.
7. Emil Brunner, *Christianity and Civilization* (Scribners, New York, 1948), p. 76.

On the other hand, we advance an observation which reinforces the preceding question: namely, that this largely discredited automatism "possesses an economic or social meaning
more than a technical meaning,"[8] as should have been the case
if technology had truly taken up the cause of automatism.

Far from liquidating humanism, a heritage we wrongly consider imperiled by technology, the latter is today its sole reser-
voir, sole context for its rebirth, if only the ecclesial revolution
is not inhibited.

2. TECHNOLOGY AND THE DIONYSIACS OF THE BODY

A. From Technology to Technological Civilization

It goes without saying that it is not a chronology of the development of technology which will be of prime importance here.
While not wholly meaningless, such an approach would have a
purely relative value in this context. It would only entail a matter of listing the technical object which corresponds, according
to one's romanticism or apocalypticism, to this or that scale of
values.

It is true that technology has developed in different stages,
and that its development was realized in spurts of more or less
brief duration. But to pretend that there is more than one technique would be a proposition we must regard as false at best.
Technology is one, and nothing less than technology is what
confronts man when he becomes aware of the fact that he *is* a
body as much as he *is* a soul—and the various Platonizing ter-
minologies according to which, time and again, Western man
has been told that he had a body as he had a soul are here bound
to miss the point.

---

8. Gilbert Simondon, *Du mode d'existence des objets techniques* (Aubier, Paris, 1958),
p. 11.

There can be one and only one technology.

Indeed, to say that man is a body is already to make the body something other than a tool that extends the soul; it is to make it a language; that is, man come to terms with his body—a process which is at once beyond and on this side of the body in which it takes hold, a process which means that man considered as body *is* already other than the body which he *has*. In addition, since there is no language without society, from the utopianism of the individual body to the utopianism of the social body we find ourselves in one and the same trajectory, that of a technique of the human, of the humanization of man.

Dealing at one moment with religious obedience, as in magic, at another with profane obedience, as at least apparently in the tool, in the end we are still dealing with the same technique of the human.

A number of authors, however, continue to think that there is a basic difference between the tool and technology, between what exteriorizes man and what interiorizes him. Thus, one argues that the tool, not affecting man in his inner consciousness, only extends him, while technology overcomes him completely, not without having changed him in the meanwhile.

But who can fail to see that man, hammer in hand, is no longer what he was previously? Who can deny that humanization as extension of man and humanization as alteration of man are two concomitant aspects of a single process? No more than humanization through the tool allows us to situate man closer to or within nature does language allow man to fall back into his body. And even so-called body language cannot prevent man from being lifted out of his body. Otherwise the body itself must be conceived of, like nature, as the site par excellence of counter-utopia, just as formerly the flesh was considered the seat of sin.

In beginning our definition of technology in this way, we are assured of the possibility of insisting, not only that technology is one, but also that it expresses the fundamental utopianism of the human reality. Conversely, it is one and the same utopia which is expressed through technology, whether understood as a tool or as a method, whether as a factor of the exteriorization or of the interiorization of man, whether in terms of the flesh or of the spirit. From this it follows that technology in itself is unsuited to any indulgence in an apocalyptics of the body, regardless of whatever claim is made in the field of either language or ethics by those who argue that the spells of the body, for lack of words, take the place of a pentecost of the Word. Differing from nature or history, technique, symbol of the very radicalization of utopia, means that it is not necessary for man to be doomed to death by his body; on the contrary, as the utopian horizon of a destiny, the body can even represent to man the theater of his resurrection, the prolepsis of his life. Once it is lived, the human never returns to nature, not even by means of an apotheosis of the life "lived-up" (Matt. 17:9).

There is no real difference between a hammer and a spaceship, no real difference either between the invention of fire and that of the steam engine. On the other hand, in standing upright, man makes a greater leap toward the human than when he steps onto the moon.

If, then, there is only one technique of the human, and if, whatever the framework, mythic or scientific, technology exists only from the moment when man becomes aware of embodying himself as though he were another, or insofar as he is no longer the same, then the process of humanization is no more endangered by technological civilization than it was by the messianic humanism or the humanistic naturalism of the past. Human technique can operate just as easily through technology as it did in pouring itself into the mold of nature or of history. Of course, I am not saying that with respect to human technique nothing happens when the technological phenomenon passes from the tutelage of myth to that of science; man as a technique is indeed threatened, but not by the fact that method has replaced the tool or that technology is no longer what it once was, but by the fact that technological society is still at the stage of the tool, somewhat as though we were still at the stage prior to the advent of the plow.

To recite Genesis to the four corners of the moon has not, as far as we know, brought heaven and earth, God and man, any closer—not to mention man and man. At most, it has been shown that we must not confuse mechanization and humanization, and that it is not by constantly saying: "Lord, Lord" that one enters the kingdom of heaven (Matt. 7:21). Technological civilization is, consequently, hardly more than a new test which the techniques of the human must confront, in the same way as they formerly confronted nature or history, either as myth or as ideology.

Beyond the fact that there is no more than one, technology is also neutral.[9] If it is not by definition hostile to the human, neither does technology guarantee humanization. Man has conquered nature, but only to the extent that he has had access to his own nature and has conquered it. He has intervened in the course of events, but solely to the extent that he has had access to, and been steward of, his own freedom. Likewise, he will have truly mastered technology only when and to the extent that, no longer confined within his body as in a prison, he will finally be able to live it as event of the resurrection. Lacking this—and it can already be observed in the preponderant place given the body in soap advertisements and other baptismal ersatzes, in the practice of yoga diverted from its spiritual ends by the adepts of new and exclusively somatic practices—there is no doubt that instead of a liberation of the body in the fire of the Spirit, we will have little more than fireworks. Let us not be surprised, then, in the meanwhile, that in moving from biotechnics to theology by way of every manner of mystical somersault, the very notion of body enjoys such a notoriety that it becomes rather stale, and that, as on the morrow of Easter, we can no longer imagine how man can become an integral part of himself unless he is raised from the dead.

Having insisted on the singleness of technology, highlighted its neutrality, and stressed the importance of its assisting the passage from man to the human, have we now contradicted our thesis of the decline of myth and the emergence of the technological phenomenon? We think not, for the simple reason that technology, even when it is no longer rudimentary, in general still belongs more to the universe of myth than to that of technique. It is this backwardness which more than anything else handicaps the ecclesial revolution and becomes an obstacle to

---

9. Cf. Georges Friedmann, *La Puissance et la Sagesse* (Gallimard, Paris, 1970), p. 23.

the utopianism of the technological phenomenon in itself. Whatever the case, if technology alters its status in moving from myth to technique, we are dealing, in what concerns man, with one and the same technique, despite the circumstances—and likewise, depending on the circumstances, we change universes.

While mythology gives us the impression of our being present at an *inventory* of the world, technology for its part gives us the impression of being present at the very *invention* of the world. Myth seeks to say something, even to reveal something, and whatever the thing may be, mythology *represents* it. Technique *reproduces* it. Discovery is what interests technology. The symmetry between myth and technique nonetheless underlines their difference: in searching for the Indies, America is discovered; leaving from *here,* one could arrive *nowhere else* but *there.* Likewise, the symmetry between representation and reproduction no less accentuates their difference: in order for there to be representation, myth must reabsorb every *novum* by drawing it into an *initium,* a beginning of beginnings; eventually, it must reduce every notion of creation to the level of a myth of origins, of an absolute *already* whose outcome is realized by the apocalypticism of the *not yet.*

But in order for there to be reproduction, the key notion of creation must in particular be released from the yoke exercised by every myth of *the* origins. To speak of reproduction is to imply above all that where there is no origin of origins, no original, no prototype, there can only be creation and that, as a consequence, humanization still remains possible. Even in the book of Genesis, creation does not designate some origin of origins;[10] rather, it indicates an investing of meaning in that which was devoid of meaning. In fact, no one would ever be tempted by the thought that in conceiving of man as a creature, Genesis made a robot out of him, turned him into some machine to be domesticated. On the contrary, Genesis simply relates the fact that humanization can only be realized in displacing the human, in freeing it *from* as well as *for* nature, which thereby enters into the field of the human. When we speak of

---

10. When God began to create, the earth was without form and void (Gen. 1:1–2).

creation we are in fact speaking of humanizing the man who is a stranger to the human. That is why nature appears as a power of man, a technique, since man, far from being expelled by nature, inserts himself into it.

Inserting the human into that which is not human, inserting the human into that which is foreign to it is what is at stake in the techniques of the human—what is at stake, too, in techno-logical society. As Simondon writes: "Total culture is what per-mits us to discover the alien as human." To which he adds that "the machine . . . is the alien in which the human is enclosed."[11] Ellul is saying nothing different when he does his utmost to show that technology today is no longer simply a means but that it takes form and integrates itself into the very rationality of the social body,[12] a rationality whose structure it has beforehand modified rather profoundly.

Technology is therefore not reproved for its rationality, or for the six other capital sins (artificiality, automatism, self-augmen-tation, monism, universalism, autonomy) which only constitute the other side of the coin, as Ellul himself would not deny, having very judiciously diagnosed their otherwise extremely insidious threat. Technology is reproved for the way in which it shakes and challenges the kind of cumulative rationality to which our previous techniques of the human had accustomed us. In sum, when technology is reproved for denaturing man and, under the cover of rationalization (for efficiency, declares Ellul, is not always synonymous with choice), for leading man to abdicate freedom, if not history or reason itself, technology is actually reproved for allegedly abusing man in forcing the human to cast off all its moorings in a tradition of anthropocen-tric rationality.

B. *Homo Technicus et Religiosus*

Let us note, however, that such a reproval is not necessarily an indication of some kind of myopia—far from it. And we must

---

11. Simondon, p. 9.
12. Jacques Ellul, *The Technological Society* (Knopf, New York, 1964).

acknowledge that the intransigence of an Ellul, lucid from beginning to end, renders greater service to clarification and comprehension of the debate than the apocalyptic delirium of a Skinner[13] or the beatific enthusiasm of a Toffler.[14]

Basically, the debate concerns the question of whether humanization can only be realized, as was thought until now, by means of more or less anthropocentric prejudices or, conversely, whether abandoning these prejudices will guarantee humanization. On the one hand, with Ellul, it is not so much a theory that one obstinately tries to safeguard, as the dignity of man. On the other hand, with the help of science, one theory runs the strong risk of prevailing, but not without having thrown man overboard in the process.

Taking sides with neither of these positions, we plead for a third way.

In order to disengage and better define our option, let us point out to begin with that this new attack against anthropocentrism today is in great part motivated by the striking repercussions of contemporary scientific thought. From the latter, in fact, are derived the data on which this attack is based. An attack aimed, in opposition to what is held as sedimentary anthropologism, at showing the importance of the fact that man, even though or perhaps because he is an unknown, remains nonetheless quantifiable. A datum of nature, man in such a perspective would become a datum of consciousness, a mathematical datum; this is an allegation which, we must admit, progressively gathers strength to the extent that data processing and cybernetics take up the slack of myth and, particularly, of the modern ideology of irresistible progress.

Now, if we look closely, this ideology itself cannot help but appear to be a result of the secularization of the classical notion of providence, a secularization previously perpetrated under the direct or indirect influence of Bacon and Descartes. What is important to note here is that the anthropocentrism under which the myth of progress still appeared or, for that matter, the ideology that flowed from this myth, was in fact due to an optical

---

13. B. F. Skinner, *Beyond Freedom and Dignity* (Bantam, New York, 1972).
14. Alvin Toffler, *Future Shock* (Random House, New York, 1970).

illusion, an illusion all the more aberrant in that, neither more nor less, one mistook divine providence for a mechanism of nature.[15] So that the myth of progress ends, all by itself, by denaturing both nature and human nature. In comparison, cybernetics has every opportunity to liberate the two from the mechanistic servitude to which they had been subjected by an allegedly naturalistic view of obedience to progress.

As strange as this may seem, anthropocentrism has been more detrimental to the human cause than we imagined, to such an extent that we would presently abandon this cause if, thanks to the complicity of preconceived notions and badly grounded opinions, we postponed the agonizing reappraisal directly concerning it. Ellul himself would not object: a social order can be imposed from without for a time, but a civilization cannot, at least not as long as man can still say "no" to such a constraint. Besides, technological civilization is no more imposed by constraint than were any of the previous civilizations. But it will not be truly able to draw us into its orbit until we have agreed to set ourselves free from every mechanistic understanding of both nature and human nature. Meanwhile, we can at least rejoice if technology, in order to be less conspicuous if not forgiven, at last takes its distance precisely vis-à-vis the mechanistic conception of the universe and its concomitant anthropocentrism. At all events, it is quite possible that the irreversibility of the technological phenomenon will prove to be more beneficial than harmful to man.

So Georges Friedmann can write with accuracy: "The technological adventure constrains man to invent new styles of life, to discover a new meaning for his life: [namely,] invention, a discovery which is translated on the practical level by choices."[16] Many years earlier, spurred on by an intuition which had not wholly deceived him, Berdyaev himself wrote in this connection that technology exercised a twofold influence on the moral and social life of man. On the one hand, he said, it pares down its spiritual character to the advantage of a more materialistic,

---

15. William Leiss, "The Domination of Nature," in *Meaning in History,* ed. Karl Löwith (University of Chicago Press, Chicago, 1949), pp. 4–9.
16. Friedmann, p. 404.

more mechanistic conception of life. On the other hand, he pointed out, technology is likewise characterized by an aptitude that pushes man to free himself from both materialism and the flesh, and provides the spirit with the possibility of expanding its field of freedom.[17] This is true, but we find ourselves in the situation of not knowing which saint to turn to. It is true, but it is neither more nor less plain than the nose on one's face.

For it is evident that as vector of a technique of the human, technology is neither more nor less materialistic, neither more nor less spiritualistic, than any other previous vector. It is not the vector that one should object to but the fallout, the still noxious repercussions of antiquated techniques of the human. As for automatism, which, as Simondon says correctly, represents "a fairly low degree of perfection,"[18] it is more appropriately handled in connection with the technique of the human rather than, as Ellul seems inclined to do, in connection with technology. For instance, when Ellul contends that one cannot exonerate technology simply by blaming those who make bad use of it, and that there is, consequently, only one way of making use of it,[19] he feigns ignorance of the haste with which he becomes caught in a puzzle where, moreover, he takes an evil delight in playing with the solution.[20] To pretend that all bets are down in a technological society and that all man has to do is to consent to his loss of freedom of choice is tantamount, not only to falling into a twofold misapprehension, but to feigning one's own ignorance of it as well. It is indeed unimaginable that Ellul could have forgotten what weight the famous Pyrénées of Pascal can bring to bear on this no less famous freedom of choice. It is unthinkable that he does not appeal in this regard to the argument he utilizes with his usual dexterity and perspicacity in connection with the sacred, and that he does not admit that, if technology does not eliminate the sacred but displaces it, neither does it eliminate ethics, but displaces it as well. The condition of irreversibility is the price technological civilization

---

17. Nicolas Berdyaev, *The Destiny of Man* (Harper and Brothers, New York, 1960).
18. Simondon, p. 11.
19. Ellul, *The Technological Society*, pp. 75 ff.
20. Ellul, *The New Demons.*

must pay. And, because it is still in embryo, this civilization is both victim and executioner, wounded as it is by a cultural revolution of which, under the circumstances, it happens to be the theater of operations.

But we must bring some clarifications to bear here.

First of all, in order to grasp the twofold displacement of the religious which, as I have just said, affects both ethics and the sacred, we need only refer to various manifestations in daily life. A few indications, taken on the fly, will be more than sufficient. I do not know what fate the future reserves, in the context of a technological civilization, for the Jesus freaks and other crazies for Jesus. While the church loses members, the more marginal Christian groups seem to spring up like mushrooms. They enjoy such an exuberance that in a country like France, which has developed a tough skin in such matters following a long tradition of anticlericalism, one cannot help but pay attention. In any case, religion seems to have deserted the altar, the better to invade the theater and come up with a full house. It is as if, in recent years, whatever may have been the irresistible motive which has breathtakingly accelerated the secularization of Constantinian civilization, man could not resign himself to leaving the sacred behind. It is easy enough to secularize, time and again, a religion which serves here as a support or a vehicle of the human; there, the sacred will surge forth inevitably. One is only changing religion, while it is a question of changing man —and only faith can accomplish that. As we can see today in what is called sexual liberation, we only short-circuit the displacement of ethics and the sacred by very simply converting ethics into the sacred and the sacred into ethics.

Let me explain further. First of all, it is enough to recall how sociologists (not all of them, it is true), grasping for man, naked and without the paraphernalia of convention, have tried to make us believe that ethics, all things considered, could only be defined in terms of the facts and deeds of a society in a given context. But describe it as you will, a given context can only be a received context. Take our own, for example. It is a context we inherit not only by secularizing Christian morality but also by realizing that no so-called lay morality could any longer escape this same secularization. What a pitiable context! Indeed, even more pitiable is the society which would like to live within it according to would-be "norms" of an ethics without morality, resting on the sheer claim that anyone could do openly what we formerly knew everyone did in secret. (Note in passing that a certain kind of dissent is much less the expression of utopian purpose than merely the negation of a morality which, in any case, has already discredited itself.) In short, with the help of physiological technology, there was nothing left but the step which consisted in secularizing sex so that it would become the sacralizing instrument of an ethic itself previously secularized. Besides, even if men do what they do, and do so without trying to gain even an acre of heaven, yet they do so in order to satisfy the feeling, diffuse as it may be, that man nonetheless has yet to fulfill himself. It is possible that an ethic without values can exist. But there can be no secularization without values, no technique of the human which does not allow the appearance of the human as a value added to man.

One can secularize ethics; but there is no ethics which is not a vehicle for the sacred. One can change one's religion; but only faith lets us triumph over this total religiosity for which man is at once victim and executioner. One can hold as sacred now this, now that; but it is only through faith—and not by means of some automatism of the sacred or of a technology without morality, or the two at the same time as is perhaps the case in the current sexual explosion—that man can dispose of either the world, without degrading or destroying it, or the body, without violating or profaning it. As to the body, it is doomed to death, and accordingly every experience of the human which breaks loose from the body, and is thereby limited to self-experience, is rather apocalyptic. In denouncing it, obviously what is advocated is neither old asceticism of the body through its mortification, nor on another level the refusal of the world through its negation. What is advocated is simply an attitude of faith, a mode of faith Bultmann correctly designates by the term *Entweltlichung* (desecularization). It consists in conceiving of ethics, in keeping with such a faith, as a "crisis" (in the sense of the Greek word *krisis*), as a "critique" aiming at a world worth its integration into the field of man's freedom and his destiny, that is to say, worth a "leap" from man to the human, a leap

109

which, for example, the prodigal son accomplishes when he returns to his father. Or else, by converting ethics into the sacred and, reciprocally, the sacred into ethics, we may achieve a teacup revolution of ethics only to short-circuit the revolution, if not the conversion of man. And there is the true problem, there is what is truly at stake in a technological civilization: the reconversion of man to the human.

This problem does not come from technology, even if one must have recourse to technology in order to delineate a problem which is basically religious. In this respect, we must bear in mind that, as a vector of the human, technological civilization does not behave any differently from the other vectors which have preceded it; like them, it leaves wide open the chasm between religion and faith, between the old and the new man, between the man for whom ethics is fundamentally apocalyptic or even a technique of salvation and the man for whom ethics, far from thus serving to sacralize the world, changes it into the event of the kingdom of God. Undoubtedly fatal to all traditional forms of religiosity, including the mythological religiosity of Christianity, technological culture should not—such, at least, is to be concluded from our analysis—show itself to be more allergic to the eschatology of the Christian faith than was the syncretistic technique of the imperial sacrality of Rome. There is nevertheless a condition attached: namely, that this eschatology not allow itself to be seduced or trapped by the fascinating exuberance of that consumers' religiosity which communications technology has already set in motion and which begins to unfurl with an art as appealing as, by contrast, the insidious dominating ideology is infatuated with atheism, with secularism. For if the technological problem is a religious problem it is at least partly because technology alone cannot resolve it. It does not follow, however, that Christianity must abdicate to the religious claims of this problem any more than it must be trapped by any religiosity whatsoever, under the pretext that nothing which is religious and thus puts man into question is by definition alien to Christianity. Indeed, by stubbornly refusing to associate itself with the cult of the emperor, primitive Christianity showed that it was possible to resist the mythology of the sacred which could otherwise have enclosed it. But by being accused of athiesm, which at the time was the equivalent of being accused of utopianism, Christianity did not hesitate, in its social involvement or in its eschatological understanding of faith, to challenge the social as well as the religious order of things.

Of course, it is not necessary for dissent to be accompanied by contempt. Rendering to Caesar what belongs to Caesar, the Christian involves himself in the world and challenges it all the more radically in that in the same movement he seeks to render to God what belongs to God. I do not know that Christianity ever systematically held in contempt the crepuscular religiosity of the Roman Empire on the basis that the imperial mythology of the sacred offended the holiness of the one God.

Whatever the sacralizing system of religiosity, mythological or technological, faith cannot and must not allow itself to despise the garb of religiosity in which men, obeying one fashion in order to reject another just as categorically, clothe themselves with the sole purpose of better enriching the questions which confront them. It was by not holding the emperor in contempt while simultaneously challenging his cult that Christianity was led to elaborate the trinitarian doctrine of God as ground of the principle of religious iconoclasm and the political involvement of the believer. It is true that in order to link involvement to protest and protest to involvement, one had to be wary of drowning faith in religiosity, as do some of our contemporaries, like Harvey Cox,[21] who seem to advocate it under the pretext of playing the Good Samaritan.

With this reservation, and holding to it without succumbing to the siren's song, perhaps the eschatic logic of the Christian faith will be able to fertilize the utopianism of the omnidirectional religiosity through which a technological civilization, in search of a sacrality proper to it, is still feeling its way. And perhaps, too, it will be able to control an overfull civilization, for want of being able to bathe it in the fullness.

---

21. Harvey Cox, *The Feast of Fools* (Harvard University Press, Cambridge, 1964); Ellul, *The New Demons*, likewise denounces this tendency.

3. FROM THE MYTHOLOGY OF THE SACRED TO THE UTOPIANISM OF TECHNIQUE

All that dies is merely technique.

Destined to death, even the body is a technique which would crush man and expel him if language did not turn the body into the very instrument of the reign of man, if it did not make a kingdom of the body.

But, bound to the body, language returns to it, ineluctably, just as man returns to the dust from which he is formed; in its turn, language turns into a technique in which the word itself stiffens as soon as it gives way to the "myth of the word," and writing up the word *(scriptura)* is transformed into words written down *(scripta),* into a corpus of received texts.

Body, language, word: we rediscover this triad or its variants in all techniques of the human, that is to say, in every instrument which mediates the passage from man to the human. The most intimate expression of the body, language is not concerned only with the order of words; it reflects likewise the order of the world,[22] that is, the human as a space for divine transcendence. Language nudges the body into the word as well as anchoring the word in the body, even as the imaginary is anchored in the real. Indeed, there is no utopia except in terms of the realizable, and the imaginary is nothing other than a utopianism of the real. In bespeaking the body, it is therefore the utopianism of the human reality which the word seeks to express through language.

A. The Profane and the Sacred

In a universe dominated by mythology, it is through religion (either as reading or decoding, or as compilation or information processing) that this utopian function of language is fulfilled. The two foci of such a religion are then constituted on the one

---

22. Georges Gusdorf, *Science et foi* (S.C.E., Paris, n.d.), p. 26.

hand by the profane and on the other by the sacred. But profane and sacred do not yet characterize elements which are mutually opposed or exclusive. They constitute rather the two foci of an ellipse, where religion, if it has an occasional tendency to colonize the profane in the name of an *imperium* of the sacred, has essentially no other purpose than to "secularize" the sacred, to make it worldly, to domesticate it by pushing even further back the frontiers of the profane *(profanum,* that which leads to the sacred and therefore is distinct from it), and, finally, to let its utopian space become a dwelling place for man. It is only later, when religion turns into "technique" (in the bad sense of the term) that sacred and profane lose their solidarity. They become dislocated and split from one another to the extent that they reach the point of opposing and excluding each other. Their respective trajectories situate them, then, in orbits whose phases differ from one another, so much so that the harmony of the world finds itself broken. Religion, then, has nothing else to do but ready itself for its own secularization and dishabilitation, a secularization and a dishabilitation which are pursued with so much desperation that one is bound soon to wake up realizing that the very instrument for the demise of religion is itself wielded in a manner rather religious. To be sure, the result is hardly ever anything more than a kind of religiosity boomerang. For two reasons: on the one hand, because it is merely the effect of a kind of backlash resulting from a religion now obsolete; on the other, because one cannot secularize everything without falling into the trap of sacralizing everything. Any religiosity which boomerangs destroys itself; it confuses iconoclasm and suicide: religion, as it were, would only consist in "secularizing" the sacred. Bent on negating itself, it is a counter-religion, a religious automatism which lacks precisely that which the body cannot replace in engulfing itself, nor even the word reduce to silence in exiling itself; it is an automatism which lacks language. Nor is it surprising, under these conditions, for everything to be profane (secular, as we put it today) or for everything to be sacred, and for "future shock" to settle by giving rise to a tower of Babel.

Variants of the basic triad—body, language, word—whose dynamics we have just sketched briefly are at work at various levels of the biblical universe and at various depths of the utopian horizon of Christianity. For example, with respect to the biblical universe, we can cite the incarnation and its two foci, creation and pleroma. Likewise, *novum* and *eschaton* can be cited as foci of *kairos*. Nor are analogous triads lacking in the Christian tradition. Here, it is the Gospel which serves as language and, at the same time, mediator between tradition and church on the one hand, and the world (social body) and the church (body of Christ) on the other. But it is not necessary to extend such a list. What gives the technique of the human this character of triadic composition is precisely its utopianism, and also, in particular, the fact that it seeks to avoid all the false alternatives of binary composition, where man is supposed to choose between this world and the next, between the horizontal and the vertical, between the profane and the sacred, between the beginning of beginnings and the end of ends. But this is not all. There are still two more items to which we must turn our attention.

We have already alluded to the first. It refers to the doctrine of the trinity, a doctrine which for various and, occasionally, clearly bad reasons has been said to be the Christian doctrine par excellence. Let us point out in passing that it is triadic not only *ad extra* but also *ad intra,* in itself; so much so that Feuerbach (a theologian manqué to the extent that he was the gravedigger only of a Christianity locked into an ideology) did not miss out on the opportunity to emphasize that it was precisely the trinity that gave God a human face.[23] Not only does the trinity prevent man from being confused with God, it also prevents God from being foreign to man. God is the radically other: that is, not the one who fills up the lacunae of language but the one who shatters space to such an extent that God and Word are henceforth synonyms, and it is no longer "it" but God who speaks, it is no longer I but the Spirit who speaks, and it is no longer someone dead who supposedly comes back to life but Christ who has risen. In short, if it is by means of the doctrine of the trinity that the church has thwarted the apotheosis of

---

23. Ludwig Feuerbach, *The Essence of Christianity,* trans. George Eliot (Peter Smith, 1958).

man, though he be the emperor, it is in addition through an ecclesial revolution that this doctrine of the trinity has passed into the facts of life and has been translated into man's daily realities. Not that subsequently one will never be able to ask whether, how, and in what sense emperors or other Christian kings can actually differ from Caesar Augustus. The fact is that in the meantime Christianity has become less trinitarian than monotheistic. And indeed, in the nineteenth century Schleiermacher goes so far as to say, rather paradoxically, that what characterizes Christianity is not so much theism as monotheism.[24] The Roman authorities, for their part, had not been mistaken when they very simply promulgated the dissolution of Christianity *(vos non licet esse)*. What they objected to was not that it was theistic or monotheistic. They criticized it for fomenting, in fact, a political utopianism which countered and undermined the order of things, the status quo, simply because it was based on an eschatological understanding of man.

The second thing to which we must turn our attention concerns the trinity as a constitutive element of a *doxa*. We hesitate to mention it here because so much of what is doctrine has today fallen into disrepute. And yet we do not in the least fear to bathe ourselves in computer science, cybernetics, genetic codes, and the like, even to the point of being both brainwashed and deluded by these things. The difference between the more or less metaphysical god of the early Christians and the more or less metamechanistic god of our techno-biostructures is that formerly the question of meaning, draining the entire utopian space of man, was bound up with—the word is appropriate—the *technique* of a language about God; and that today, for lack of being able to *name* God,[25] this very question no longer tends to dissolve itself in the technique of a language for which body and word, while referring to each other, remain nevertheless distinct, but rather tends to dissolve itself in the language of a

---

24. Friedrich Schleiermacher, *Der Christliche Glaube* (1849); *The Christian Faith* (1928). Even if excellent in other respects, the book of H. Richard Niebuhr, *Radical Monotheism and Western Culture* (1960), displays a no less symptomatic title.
25. Cf. André Dumas, "Dieu, pourquoi, comment?" *Bulletin du Centre Protestant d'Etudes*, June 1973.

technique of the body, in a body language aiming moreover at a technique of the divine (which is not without bearing on the revival of occultism and of astrology or on the confusion of the sacred and the profane), suggesting that to a certain extent Ellul is right when he calls utopia "the negro spiritual" of modern Western intellectuals, their consolation in the face of their slavery, and their escape from something they are unable to prevent.[26] Whatever the case, even this very characteristic way of Ellul's of buying utopia combines, whether we like it or not, to reinforce a position which allows us to recall that the technological problem is essentially a religious problem. And with this reiteration we conclude these remarks on the universe marked by a mythological orientation of techniques of the human, in order now finally to examine what happens when we consider these in terms of another universe, no less homogeneous to them, which we call a universe dominated by technology.[27]

B. More Than Profane and Less Than Sacred

In a technologically oriented universe, it so happens that the schema we have proposed is scarcely modified. On its main points it persists without exhibiting changes that would upset its general orientation. The fact remains that for want of established religion, it is the *religious* which will now assume the utopian function of language. Between religion and the religious the difference is not, so to speak, a question of degree, as

---

26. Ellul, *The New Demons*, p. 177.
27. We could have said "scientific"; but we have opted for "technological" in spite of the risks of ambiguity (which we want to avoid as much as possible) that the term will cause in the present context of our argument. Two kinds of reasons compel us. First of all, it is not unimportant to note that at the root of this term there is the Greek word *techne* which designates an activity pervaded with religiosity. On the other hand, rather than opposing the two conceptions of technology, we are trying to emphasize their kinship by including under the same purview technology as the application of science and technology (also called technique and serving to designate, for example, technological society) as the domain of which science has become an "element," a "means" (M. Mauss, quoted by Ellul, *The Technological Society*, p. 10). Let us also add that if the euphony of the parallelism mythological/technological is somewhat irresistible (yet not without good reason), one cannot accuse myth or technique of encroaching upon one another; this has not always been the case in the relationship of myth (whose vocation is essentially religious) and science.

all those who opt for Dionysus over Apollo seem to think, giving the impression that one must be "way out" in order to be "in." No, between religion and the religious there is the difference that arises in the passage from *mythos* to *logos,* from "sayings" to "saying," from saying things to saying the word, a saying which would already present itself as a *doing,* at least virtually. If one could say that religion is essentially passion, one can also say then that the religious is above all action. The religious consists in deeds, and, as in a play, it must be acted out. It re-presents. Or, as was said previously, it *reproduces.*

For all that, the religious is not without hearth or home. To be sure, it will still be distinct from religion as far as the dialectic put into play between the profane and the sacred is concerned. But this dialectic will not be upset even if, at first, it is shaken in its foundations as if to make a clean sweep. Without wanting to insinuate that religion favors, that it opts for, what is stable and permanent in a tradition, the profane and the sacred nevertheless serve as stabilizing instruments for it. On the other hand, we will have to consider a mixture of the profane and the sacred when we discuss the religious and that which would serve as "fuel" for it. Notwithstanding the prophetic nature of the religious, it emerges above all as an exigency of totality according to which either everything is profane or sacred or else nothing is either profane or sacred. The reality, however, is far less complex. For man does not live by science alone. Science is centripetal, turned in on itself; while life, which is open to the world, acknowledges no other reason for itself than that which does not hypertrophy or pare down utopia. Also of the same order is the difference between the religious and religion, the flanks of which—I mean, religion—are wisely protected by the profane and the sacred. Of these, the religious is surely not totally divested. Indeed, where religion would see only the profane, the religious sees more than the profane; it sees there what today, whether rightly or wrongly, is called the secular.[28] And

---

28. Since Raymond Aron and following Jacques Ellul, we have had no trouble in speaking of secular religions, as if, retrospectively, the religions of the past were not secular also but were only religious. Unless, of course, it be admitted, as I am suggesting, that for these same religions the secular was already more than the profane.

similarly, at the other extreme, the religious sees only the sacral, something less than the sacred, precisely where religion would be disposed to see the sacred. By means of the sacred the reality of God weighs on the entire order of things, occasionally to the point of encumbering it and thus settling the price which must be paid for the attempt to *name* God.[29] Not that the sacral tries to be spared from the divine; but it is not burdened with God or shaken by him. Should the sacral set itself in motion, it would only be because, deliberately keeping from naming God, it would be satisfied with dancing out his total inconspicuousness. Formerly, one had to snatch God from idolatry; today, as Bultmann and later Ellul and Dumas have remarked, he must be delivered from anonymity. But today, as before, it is a matter of naming God. It is a matter, to put it in theological terms borrowed from the tradition and in the sense that Bultmann gives them, of knowing how it can happen that one speaks *of* God while knowing oneself condemned to speak only *about* God.

C. Saying, Doing, Meaning

We can permit ourselves a generalization here which La Palisse would not have disowned. It was not so long ago that one could only be born either a Platonist or an Aristotelian. Likewise, there were those for whom God could only elude everything that one claimed could be said of him. And, on the other hand, there were those for whom one could not speak about God without speaking of him. On the one hand, if he exists, God remains ungraspable, ineffable. He is the unknown God of those Athenians whom Saint Paul encountered in the Areopagus. On the other hand, God is the one of whom Pascal said that one would not seek him if one had not already found him.

Perhaps it is only a matter of the two faces of God. But we would still be dealing with two irreconcilable conceptions: on the one hand, the absolutist conception of God; on the other, the eschatological conception of God. It is true that within the

---

29. On *homo laborans,* see André Dumas, *Prospective et prophétie* (Les Editions du Cerf, Paris 1972).

framework of a technological problematic, the diversity of antagonistic if not irreconcilable conceptions of God is inscribed in the very core, in the very code, of the technological phenomenon—that is to say, in the *logos* which, as it is substituted for the *mythos,* drains and compresses the universe of the *technè* and substitutes the fact of "saying" for the "thing to be said," the fact of saying being itself constitutive of both the organ of its own rationality and the given of its own objectivity. Could it be that the *logos* is itself made up of two sides which ignore one another—or try to?

The fact remains that one is thus allowed to be tempted by the distinction which can be formulated with the help of the two classical approaches taken by Western civilization concerning, on the one hand, the specifically Greek contribution and, on the other hand, the specifically Hebraic one; on the one hand, the *ratio,* a framework of understanding particularly polarized by reason, even including reason as the final form of the apocalypse, reason as in the apocalypticism of Hegel or again as the omega point of Teilhard de Chardin; on the other hand, the incarnation, a framework of understanding polarized neither by the absolute as God, nor by the absolute as man, but focused on "saying" as eschatological discourse, in such a way that the *logos* which becomes incarnate cannot be reduced to a "saying" that would be constitutive of itself, let alone of itself as that which is said, as *fatum* (that which is written), but in such a way that the *logos* referring no longer to a "saying" which would already be a "doing" now refers to a "meaning," a *scriptura* (that which remains to be written, the unheard of, the *novum* in opposition to the *scripta* which are only received texts).

Locked into saying the thing, myth has nothing else to do than *speak* the work of God; and if God is sometimes conceived as creator, it is rather with the features of a demiurge that he is most often presented.

On the other hand, locked into doing the word, it is by silence that the *logos* is threatened, whether it be through some *anankè* which locks man in the *cosmos* or (as is the case today by means of a sort of devolution of Christian values which is accompanied at least in appearance by a resurgence of Greek dionysiacs) by replacing, in the mythological schema of language as mediator

119

of body and word, the utopianism of the latter by the a-topianism of the dance. In the latter case, one moves at the same time from the body as temple of the spirit to the spirit as temple of the body (1 Cor. 6:19), from the body as event of the resurrection to the resurrection as event of the body. What is missing in this dialectic of the dance and the body (the dance as tautology par excellence and the body as the failing of gods doomed to silence) is nothing other than a *liturgy,* a meaning. In spite of appearances, dionysiac disembodiment is simply a logical positivism at the level of the body, a positivism of body language.

Thus, as *ratio,* the *logos* ends up dizzied by its own discourse and, lacking meaning, can only dance it; it is as incarnation that the *logos* can rise to liturgy. One becomes aware of it immediately: liturgy does not seek to underestimate either dance or discourse, any more than it consents to bridle the body. It is wary of making up for the dislocation of the body with the immanence of the dance, or for the disarticulation of language with the fatalistic automatism of a discourse without end.

D. *Orans, Laborans, Collaborans*

We have found that in the final analysis the problematic of myth culminated in a scission, a schism between the profane and the sacred. It is an analogous dualism that one rediscovers at the end of our inquiry of the problematic of the *logos* as *ratio.* Yet, we have also found that it is on the refusal of the cleavage in which myth fails that the problematic of the *logos* takes its thrust. And we now point out that if the dialectic of the profane and the sacred breaks apart under the effect of a sclerosis of the utopianism which is inherent in it, it is under the effect of the hypertrophy of the same utopianism that the dialectic of the secular and the sacral similarly breaks apart. We should not be surprised at this. In passing from one regime to another, we do no more than witness a kind of permutation of the roles between God and man, and this to the extent that "doing" passes from God's hands to man's. At least, one moves from *homo orans* to *homo laborans*,[30] from the man of prayer to the man at work, without excluding, however, one from the other; and, the conception of God changing itself concomitantly, one moves from a conception of God as creator, even as demiurge, to one of God as the word which becomes incarnate itself or accounts for the *raison d'être* of all that is.

But it is obvious that, on the level of symbols, when we move from *orans* to *laborans* a transition takes place which is realized by a polarization that favors the *deed* to the detriment of *language*. And, conversely, when we move from the creator to the word, the transition which is effected favors *language* to the detriment of the *deed*.[31]

Now, there are two faces to the *logos* which we must take into account.

What we have just said concerning *homo laborans* emerges from the cycle of the *logos* understood as *ratio*. Carried away by his technique, *homo laborans* is bogged down in the this-worldly, in the immanence and the positivism of his works. To parody a famous saying, he "knows how the earth turns," but in the end is stumped by the question of "how one returns to the earth," and why.

But it is only when one considers things under the other aspect of the *logos* and when one sees them in the perspective of the incarnation that our problem changes its face. In fact, in the logic of incarnation, distinguished from *ratio* as well as from *mythos* while at the same time advocating their respective causes, it is at one and the same time as *orans* and as *laborans* that man conceives of himself and thereby appears under the even more human aspect of *homo collaborans:* not merely as God's mouthpiece or his "labor" but rather as his co-worker (1 Cor. 3:9).

---

30. On this last point, a comparison of the Athanasian creed and the counter-creed of Lucky in Samuel Beckett's *Waiting for Godot* could not be more illuminating. In the first case, the utopianism of language set off by a series of *et tamen* is realized by bringing about an eschatological celebration of the Word: God breaks into the silence of man. In the second, he is caught in the wild rhythms of words dancing the opaque thickness of their silence—a silence in which God himself is sunk.
31. Saint Augustine, *Confessions*, 10. 6. 10.

E. From the Sacred to Utopia: Liturgy

What can we say? First of all, that God is not the absolute of this or that, of language or act, but the creator who speaks and it is done, the redeemer who acts and whose word remains. He is the God who comes and whose reality is brought about by the human reality. Consequently, this being a question of the otherness of God, of the condition *sine qua non* of naming God, it amounts to saying that this condition is no more facilitated by the categories of thought by which the mythological universe is articulated than it is impaired by those of a technologically oriented universe: it is no more facilitated by language as technique of "saying" than it is broached by technique as the language of "doing." For there exists a third way, that of "meaning," where language and act, the imaginary and the real, do not mutually eclipse one another but are mutual supports of one another. This is the way par excellence used in the liturgy, since it is at once language of the body and its metamorphosis, silence of the word and its pentecost, common action of the people (according to the etymology of the word) and *vox populi vox dei,* work of man and work of God. It is not by accident that if the church arises as the body of the dead and risen Christ, it is through the liturgical act of the word made flesh that the alpha and omega of the eschatological discourse—i.e., the Son of man bringing about the reign of God—come into play. In other words, it is not by accident that, once it is understood as eschatic existence, faith issues in a politics of man, and that it presents itself as a technique of the human whose qualities encompass, while surpassing, the characteristics by which we have just acknowledged each of the techniques of the human that are worked out either within some clear and sharp framework of religion or in terms of a no less demanding dynamic of the religious.

On two essential points, liturgy indeed differs equally from religion and from the religious as vectors of the human.

1. Let us take two men, said Saint Augustine; one is content with contemplating the world while the other, also contemplating, begins to question the world. They will not see two differ-

ent worlds. Very simply, the first one's approach will have made him dumb, the other's will have given him the possibility of speaking. And Saint Augustine adds that in fact the world addresses all men in the same way. Its language, however, will not be deciphered except by him who hears it through the truth that he bears in him.[32] For Saint Augustine, the world can thus present itself as silence and as word, as emptiness and as epiphany of God. Completing these two ways of seeing the world, we state, first of all, that rather than nature[33] it is religion which abhors a vacuum and seeks to fill it; then, we argue that, faced with the abundance of the world and its wastefulness, only the religious can express its ultimate and total precariousness; and, finally, we add that the liturgy, transcending the dualism of silence and word, of emptiness and overflow, is the only thing capable of anticipating the eschatological fullness of which the world is event. To be sure, it is this same fullness that the dialectic of the profane and the sacred desperately seeks to mediate but succeeds only in localizing in a world beyond this world, and that, similarly, the dynamics of the secular and the sacral attempts to mimic by playback but attains only through a reproduction of a fallen world. In the first case, it is from the scarcity of language that God arises; in the second, from the scarcity of the act. But it is a completely different matter altogether when it comes to the liturgy, and this brings us to the second point.

2. We have noted that a kind of mutation was brought about in switching from the dialectic of the profane and the sacred to the dynamics of the secular and the sacral, keeping in mind that the secular is already more than the profane and that the sacral, on the other hand, is less than the sacred—as if, in one case, God were more than God and, in the other, less than God.

In the one case, God must be snatched from idolatry, that is, from his pseudonyms; in the other, from anonymity and his homonyms. But in neither case is it possible for God to be the radically other, in relation to whom the absolute is but a misrepresentation and reason merely a misunderstanding. (Let us note

---

32. Saint Augustine, *Confessions,* 10. 6. 10.
33. Pascal, *Pensées.*

in passing that the hermeneutics of the Word and the hermeneutics of history are thus each being challenged: they reabsorb act into language and language into act.) By contrast, from an eschatological point of view, liturgy is the basis upon which language and act balance and sustain each other even while the deficiencies of the dialectic of profane and sacred and those of the dynamics of secular and sacral are corrected. How is this so? Simply in that both are received into the matrix of the *eschaton,* so that they may be given life under the respective aspects of the two eschatological *figures*[34] par excellence: the two ministries, that of the *sacrament* and that of the *Word.* The sacrament makes an event of the world of facts, an advent of God. As for the Word, it transfigures both the overflow and emptiness of the world, filling it with the fullness of God, the pleroma, and breathing in it the Spirit of Pentecost.

Unlike religion, whose sanctuary is in heaven, and the religious, for which the earth is the chapel, liturgy has no temple[35] (Rev. 21:22).

That the innerworldly dynamics of the religious can appear as an attempt to radicalize the otherworldly dialectic of religion surely is to be acknowledged if only because of the increasing relevance of this attempt and its legitimacy, at least on certain points. But then this should make it even more evident that such a radicalization is precisely what is at stake in the eschatological perspective which defines the basic orientation of liturgy. Contrary to the secular, sacrament is not something more (nor is it something less) than the profane, but an iconoclasm of the *more* that the profane would like to be (when it is set up as a homonym for God), as well as of the *less,* the level to which it fairly often falls (when it is understood as a psuedonym for God). The same can be said of the Word, whose characteristic is precisely that it pulls the world away from nature, and destiny away from history, as so many masks which one inflicts upon God. This is why only the eschatic logic of liturgy is capable of guaranteeing a technique of the human, which guards against secularism and likewise avoids the temptation of sacralism. As technique of the

---

34. Erich Auerbach, *Mimesis* (Princeton University Press, Princeton, 1953).
35. Cf. Pierre Maury, *L'eschatologie* (Labor et Fides, Geneva, 1959), p. 9.

human, only liturgy is capable of joining together language and act and between them, without a gap, of weaving the eschatological dialectic of the *logos* which becomes incarnate, a dialectic whose poles are constituted, on the one hand, by creation and, on the other, by pleroma. And the absence of a temple does not mean that as a consequence nothing is sacred or everything is sacred; it means that the sacred is above all characteristic of that which holds God and man in a reciprocal obligation which binds them to nature without enslaving them to it, and this precisely to the extent that it binds them to one another without ever confusing them with one another.

God is no demiurge, but the creator; no lifesaver, but the redeemer; no revolutionary gadget to fill the emptiness of the soul, but the spirit that gives life. In a technological civilization this kind of God is less in competition with man than is the case when God is confused with either nature or history. Is it not in reality from these kinds of constraints, rather than from the living God, that technology liberates man? If the argument has not led us astray, the only reasonable response to such a question is an affirmative one. Certainly, such considerations are utopian, but is it not at this price that techniques of the human are realizable and that, over and against all hope, they can turn man into a human? And, moreover, can there be any technology of man which is not at the same time vector of the human?

In opposing myth and technique I have simply wanted to show that the sacred no longer inhabits nature, but utopia.

Utopia differs from the universe of the "saying" which is that of myth, where nature can only say what it carries within itself, and I define utopia as the reconciliation of transcendence and immanence in a "meaning," which is the locus of an eschatology of the incarnation, that is to say, of a liturgy, a utopianism of faith.

Religion desacralizes. Faith is neither sacralizing nor desacralizing. It is iconoclastic.

VI

Church and Pleroma

1. TECHNIQUE AND THE LITURGY

There are thus those for whom technological civilization ultimately conceals the condemnation of man as man. And, at the other extreme, there are obviously the spokesmen of a civilization at long last tailored to man's measure if only because it would issue from the very hands of man. There is no point in citing names. Granted that the prophets are not necessarily all on the side of the establishment, in any case we have no intention of cross-examining them: our purpose is simply to clarify our position.

Those who rail against technology as well as those who sing its praises are in agreement at least with respect to the ingredients of technological civilization, the ingredients from which they derive the quasi-dogmatic divergence of their opinions. For both groups, these ingredients consist in those characteristics of technological civilization that would entice it toward automation and systematization, the efficient and the rational, toward the artificial, etc. In view of such elements, depending on one's commitment, the claim is made either that man is bound to be snuffed out or that his heart will beat to the rhythm of a humanity finally common to all men.

Now what can be ascertained when we examine this issue closely? We see that these ingredients, these characteristics used to dress up technological civilization are all without exception bred with a mechanistic understanding largely outdated in relation to technological civilization and, a fortiori, in relation to the appropriate technique of the human.

The truth is always far more simple. To be sure, when we move from one religious framework of understanding to the other, we can observe that some change takes place, though not to the extent of undermining the basis on which rests the possibility of discerning the religious dimension particular to each technique of the human. In every religious framework of understanding there is, so to speak, one constant and one variable, one part certainty and one part uncertainty. And, variable or uncertainty, this part sometimes expresses unrest, sometimes hope.

As far as the constant is concerned, regardless of the framework of understanding, it always designates a quantity. And usually, as everyone knows, it is precisely the specter of quantity which is evoked in relation to technological civilization. From production to consumption by way of communications, everything is allegedly conceived of today with an eye toward the masses. However, for all the fact that there are masses, we must not forget that this is not necessarily a concomitant of the technological phenomenon: India still displays a painful panorama, and soon it will be Africa, until now relatively untouched by technology. The basic point nevertheless remains that quantity belongs to the realm of certainty. But it is a certainty anchored as much in the subjective as in the objective (which does not mean that it is either objective or subjective—far from it: indeed, it defies every clear line of demarcation). We can now proceed to the following considerations:

1. The framework of understanding in terms of which nature is converted into a technique of the human is above all a metaphysical framework for which quantity, measured in terms of substance, is patterned after the model of the organism. Giving rise to evil and sin, scarcity is what challenges this substance when the latter is not totally determined. Hence it follows that the problematic proper to such a situation is resolved by a utopianism of abundance as the essential motif of man's liberation (or salvation). That is why this utopianism itself is placed under a particular sign, that of the reign of ends, whose ideal will consist either in letting man out of time, which destroys all, or in letting him into the eternal bliss of heaven, depending on whether, as with the Greeks, liberation, salvation, or abundance

127

are conceived as fruits of nature;[1] or, as with the Hebrews, they are conceived as a fruit of the creative spirit. For man, as Saint Thomas observes, is man only insofar as he realizes himself.[2] Thus the doctrine of creation is not only a "protest of faith in the trough of the wave of history,"[3] it is also a critique of the off-seasons of nature.

2. The framework of understanding in terms of which history is converted into a technique of the human is above all an ideological framework for which quantity, measured in terms of freedoms, is patterned after the model of the social contract. Here, it is reason which substitutes its reign for that of the ends, and its praise is sometimes required of folly itself. No less frustratingly than nature, history turns into *fatum*. The ideal then consists in trying to snatch history from the classical rhythm of repetition and return by investing it with an irreversible meaning, progress. From that perspective, though abundance is still a problem, it is nevertheless one which is practically unavoidable, at least when man's liberation or his salvation is conceived as the fruit of history: paradise is thus brought within reach of the earth. But this is no less the case when on the contrary history is conceived as a work in terms of which salvation liberates man and in which he is allowed to participate. The latter observation is justified, first, in view of the original blossoming of millenarianism which the official church would later try to overcome by throwing itself into an activism far more philanthropic than eschatological; and second, in view of the fairly widespread tendency to conceive of ecclesiology as the starting point for a politics of the kingdom (as is the case with Calvin), but which most often culminates in conceiving of this kingdom or this politics as a more or less definitive establishment in the world, as obliquely reflected in Wesley's saying, "The world is my parish" (well before McLuhan makes it a village). For such an establishment Vatican I provides the ideology.

---

1. Auguste Luneau,. *L'Histoire du salut chez les Pères de l'Eglise* (Beauchesnes, Paris), p. 76.
2. Cf. André Manaranche, *Y a-t-il une éthique sociale chrétienne?* (Editions du Seuil, Paris, 1969), pp. 140–41.
3. André Dumas, *Croire et douter* (Les Editions Oecuméniques, Paris/Lyon, 1971), p. 46.

Like Aeneas who, having reached Italy, no longer thought of leaving it,[4] we then transform history into fiction: a legal one, no doubt, like everything the Roman spirit engendered, but a fiction nonetheless, and a fiction according to which history, seen as neither perpetual return nor as pure unfolding, can have but one end. This end—whatever the term employed in the ideologies of left or right—resembles in every respect the "eternal sovereignty of Rome."

Perhaps it has happened almost without our knowing it: in viewing history as fiction, we may realize that in reflecting on nature as vector of the human we had, in fact, found our point of departure in viewing fiction as nature. If nature is merely a homonym of fiction, history is simply a pseudonym. And we discover its anonymity while waiting to call technological society "by a new name which the mouth of the Lord God will give" (Isa. 62:2).

3. That is why the framework of understanding in terms of which fiction is converted into a technique of the human is above all a technological framework for which quantity, measured in terms of organization, is patterned after the model of utopia. This means in the first place that, as we move from organism to organization, it is no longer quantity which is a problem, but quality. In the second place, this means that quality is no longer conceived in terms of the binomial of this world and the next (abundance of the heavenly paradise), or that of *before* and *after* (progress of the earthly paradise), but is henceforth understood to determine every mode of *hic et nunc*. It is obtained neither by Platonic escape nor by forward flight.

We have already said as much concerning the liberation of man in terms of happiness or salvation; there as here, we did so in the name of a single principle. The apostle Paul expresses this principle when he stresses that it is in the church that it is appropriate to look for those "good things which are to come," and which we usually look for in another world.

Inaccessible before the coming of Christ, Saint Paul argues, these benefits now belong to all those who are integrated into

---

4. Luneau, pp. 59–60, quoting J. Perret, *Virgile, l'homme et l'oeuvre* (Paris, 1952). pp. 98–99.

the body of Christ, the church. This also means that in Paul's eschatological perspective it is with those aspirations, spiritual or other, that we delude ourselves and thus fail to integrate this same body of Christ which should be destined to render to the world its worldliness, *hic et nunc,* here and now.

The Christian cannot renounce the world except by changing it, and by liberating himself from the false asceticism that confuses quality either with a regime of scarcity (which in the name of a heavenly abundance is imposed *on* nature) or with a regime of restrictions (which in the name of the future is imposed *on* history). Today, it is no longer only the eschatic logic of the liturgy of the body of Christ (viewed as social reality) which challenges these false asceticisms; it is also technology which, as vector of the human, dismantles the sacralized scaffolding of our prejudices.

Paul writes: "Therefore, let no one pass judgment on you in questions of food and drink or with regard to a festival or a new moon or a sabbath. These are only a shadow of what is to come; but the substance belongs to Christ. Let no one disqualify you, insisting on self-abasement and worship of angels" (Col. 2:-16–18);[5] observances, he says, "attest to an aspiration for spiritual goods which were inaccessible before the coming of Christ. Over certain parts of the pre-Christian world they were an inconstant shadow which even so bore the tidings of a body belonging to Christ. For it is in Christ alone that the *future benefits* (forgiveness, sanctification, communion with God, life) are present and accessible to believers in his body, which is the church."[6]

Yet there exists a major difference between the technological and the liturgical, between the cybernetic and the ecclesial organization of the human body. It emerges as soon as we try to designate the element—in point of fact, dance—which corresponds in the framework of fiction (that is, of technique as vector of the human) either to reason or to the reign of ends in the threefold combinations we have suggested earlier in order

5. Cf. Ch. Masson, *L'Epitre de Saint Paul aux Colossiens, Commentaire du Nouveau Testament,* vol. X (Delachaux et Niestlé, Neuchâtel, 1950).
6. Michel Bouttier, *La Condition chrétienne selon saint Paul* (Labor et Fides, Geneva, 1964), p. 77.

to identify the framework of history and that of nature. To say in effect that the body of Christ is composed neither of Jews nor Greeks, neither of slaves nor freedmen, was undoubtedly not science fiction. Yet it must have seemed so for a variety of people for whom social stratification could only represent submission to the decrees of fate. In order to arrest this submission, it was necessary in effect to have recourse to some mystical, more or less ascetic, interiorization: the body was interiorized. But in the church exactly the opposite takes place: by joining the body of Christ, man exteriorizes his own body to make it a place for the encounter with the other, though not for the conquest of the other; man is given to himself precisely in the moment that he no longer belongs to himself. That is why the New Testament characterizes the believer as a slave of Christ; not in order to sacralize slavery as a principle of social organization, but in order to affirm that there can be no social organization which is not based on a giving of one's self, and furthermore that such a giving must be more than mere lip service. Thus the church could not have changed the face of the earth if utopia had not already been conceived of as realizable in some fashion, and if fiction had not been conceived of as a technique destined to render to nature its nature, to truth its truth. But, with regard to fiction as a vector of the human, this is also where the similarity between the liturgical and the technological ends.

From the point of technology, it is through dance that man aspires to transfigure his body. Today, as in the New Testament, man's alienation is felt most acutely in terms of the body rather than on the idealistic plane of the soul. But, despite all appearances, dance only succeeds in interiorizing the body, so that dance in fact merely seems a means of preserving for the body a youthfulness—fictional or not—of which the body is irreversibly deprived, if not by age, then by the ideology of the youth culture itself. Furthermore, cultivating the body rather than the soul may also be an exercise involving the mystagogic fervor of some esoteric salvation or another. Nor should we be surprised at this. As we have already pointed out, if technology desacralizes everything, it is always to the advantage of a resurgence of the religious. The latter, in confusing the reign of ends with nature's self-immanence, makes happiness a fruit of nature; or, confusing reason with history's self-immanence, it makes destiny a fruit of history; or even, finally, confusing the human person with the body's self-immanence, it makes the soul a fruit of the body. And all of a sudden, it seems, we find ourselves once again at our point of departure in nature as a framework of understanding.

On the other hand, on the level of liturgy the body is above all an event of resurrection. This means, *first of all,* that it is through the service of his body—through his whole being and not merely through the soul or whatever inner self he could shelter from others or from everything foreign to it—that man commits himself to the service of others as well as to the service of the radically other who is God. But while in the dynamic of the dance this divine service is conceived of as a possibility of the body *per se,* this very possibility is presented in the eschatic logic of liturgy exclusively as a possibility of God.[7]

Second, this means that if dance aspires to an epiphany of God, then the resurrection of the dead, as Barth and Bultmann point out,[8] is a paraphrase for the word "God," but with this difference: if, for technology as well as for nature or for history, God constitutes the end of the human quest, here it is this very quest which God brings to an end. The eschatic existence of faith no longer depends upon the realm of the possibilities of technology any more than upon the realm of the necessities of nature or the determinisms of history.

This means, *third,* that what is living is "in no way something given, something 'natural.' "[9] For life belongs not to the retrievable, but to the futurable; it is the passage from an old to a new humanity, not from the human to the divine.[10] That is why the body is bearer only of that man who belongs to the future.

Finally, this means that in contrast to traditional, unrealizable utopias, the utopianism of the reign of God is structured in terms of the realizable. In contrast to technological utopianism,

---

7. Cf. Rudolf Bultmann, *Faith and Understanding,* I (Harper & Row, New York, 1969), pp. 40, 76–78; Karl Barth, *Die Auferstehung der Toten* (Chr. Kaiser, Munich, 1924), p. 29.
8. Ibid.
9. Bultmann, op. cit., p. 86.
10. Cf. Guy Wagner, *La Résurrection* (Les Editions du Cerf, Paris), p. 102.

where everything that is possible is necessary, the utopianism of the reign of God demands no less a "radicalization": it is a utopianism of the impossible, that is, of the *skandalon* of the cross and resurrection; of the impossible obligation to love one's neighbor as oneself—which is still another paraphrase of the radically other, God.

2. COMMUNITY OF THE HUMAN AND COMMUNITY OF THE *ESCHATON*

As a utopianism of the real, nature comes into play only from the moment that it is transformed into a vector of human nature. In the same way, history as a utopianism of the real comes into play only to the extent that it is transformed into a vector of man's freedom.

As long as nature is foreign, it is hostile to man. When man domesticates it and trusts it with his destiny, when it ceases to represent the profanation of the sacred, only then can we speak of a utopianism of nature.

It is the same with history. As long as it is alienating, it divides men into tribes and races, it divides man into men and women. When man makes it his reason for being and hoping, when it ceases to lie in the alienation of man from God, only then can we speak of a utopianism of history.

From a theological perspective it is therefore the notion of creation which seeks to express the utopianism of nature. It does so not by sacralizing or desacralizing nature, but by snatching it from the empirical dichotomy of the sacred and the profane. Similarly, it is the notion of redemption which expresses the utopianism of history, not by sacralizing or desacralizing history, but by releasing it, through the incarnation of the word, from the *fatum* of gods that die.

The utopianism of the real thus appears in the form of church, the body of Christ, and, consequently, the reality that transcends all the aborted dialectics of profane and sacred, na-

133

ture and history, and the reality which is a technique of the human as well as of the divine.

Insofar as technology is therefore a utopianism of the real, its framework differs from that of nature or of history illuminated, respectively, by the ascetic utopianism of the soul and the speculative utopianism of the spirit. It differs, in particular, by reason of its dionysiac utopianism of the body. But not to the extent of escaping the eschatic logic of faith. On the contrary: it is exactly this kind of utopianism that the Christian faith, through its notion of pleroma, is able to claim and assume for itself. To this end it must, of course, still undergo the cultural shift which alone can warrant, thanks to its eschatological conception of faith, its acceptance of this utopianism of the body —as was the case when, as Good Samaritan, it accepted the utopianism of the soul or that of the spirit. It will also have to adapt the structures of its ecclesiology to the structures of technological civilization and, to this end, learn how to free itself from those geographic and sociological structures that still encumber the social, political, and cultural reality of the church. Moreover, these two conditions are intimately linked.

A. Artificial Man

Limiting ourselves to the basic points, we find it sufficient to emphasize, as far as the first of these conditions is concerned, the two significant aspects under which the problem appears. One of these aspects concerns the preeminence of the body considered as a *quality* of human reality; the other concerns the artificial character of this very quality.

While in the context of scarcity and from the perspective of a utopianism of nature, the body is easily grasped as a quantity, if not negligible, at least fit for mortification, it is charged with personality (in the etymological sense of "mask") when it is considered from the viewpoint of history and of its utopianism of the spirit as vector of the human. But it is as an index or, rather, as an indicator of quality that the body appears as soon as we shift to the utopian context of technology.

With the shrinking of the globe, it is no longer in terms of his situation in nature nor in terms of his historical condition that man is now affected by great migrations such as once punctuated the process of humanization—migrations whether like those of migratory birds in the first instance, or those of crusaders with a holy mission in the second. Today these migrations mean the displacement of persons reduced to the status of mere manpower, destined to build neither cathedrals nor tombs, nor even public places like a forum or an agora. Quality is no longer measured by the soul or the spirit: it is now sunk in the body and is accordingly miniaturized, though not without suffering at the same time from the gigantism which hampers the social structures of contemporary man.

From Biafra to Bangladesh, from the Sahel to Latin America, every man is flesh of our flesh. It is enough for the concrete reality of man suddenly to be lived on a multinational scale (at least in the first stage, before being lived purely on a human scale) for the spiritual and material advantages of the man on the street to begin to correspond somewhat to the strictly economic advantages derived by the so-called multinationals from the technological dispersal of goods no less than of people. This is not, of course, to suggest that the church should begin to imitate these corporations, but rather that its spiritual strategy should not be bogged down in rearguard battles. Anticlerical and nearly atheist, even a village in Provence continues to present traits in which it is not very difficult to recognize the imprint of that reality we designate under the name "parish": nothing, to be sure, which would indicate a really living faith, but nonetheless something more than a simple veneer of Christianity. Yet a little oil from the Near East and a few American-style majorettes are enough to efface this imprint in the space of a few years. I do not want to denounce either the oil or the majorettes, even though perhaps the majorettes deserve it. I am merely trying to show that the church knew well enough how to embody the community of man when the thirst for the absolute was expressed in the categories of the soul or the spirit. Today it cannot be otherwise, without harming the church, now that this thirst is expressed in the categories of the body, and, like customs, religions have become practically interchangeable. They all look alike, including Christianity insofar as it is a religion, to

135

the extent that all remain tributary to a utopianism in which abundance is spiritual and scarcity material.

But the problem is becoming more complex today due to the fact that, as we move from the abundance of the soul or the spirit to the abundance and enchantment of the body, we suddenly come up against the fundamentally artificial character of the human reality. We are even somewhat discomforted when we become convinced of this. It is true that in the current state of affairs man sometimes appears as nothing more than a machine operator, as a mere auxiliary to machines; and that faced with such an "extraordinary proliferation of the artificial"[11] it becomes urgently necessary that we ask ourselves how far this proliferation can go without going too far.

Nevertheless, it is not only utopia itself which suddenly seems artificial in retrospect. We must face up to the fact and not become bitter even if, as Mounier said, "artifice is the nature of man."[12]

Furthermore, it is not clear why the artificial *should* oppose the natural and why "personality," that which is hoarded in the name of personal interest, *should not*. After all, is artifice not the space of the natural, as the field was once the space of the ploughman, or as words are still the space of language? For a sign to be a sign, is it not necessary that even in the context of nature it emerge from some convention, if not from the arbitrary?[13] And if we had to account for subjectivity, is it not almost certain that we could not do so without suspecting it of resting on a pedestal deeply immersed in artifice?[14]

There is no opposition between nature and artifice; rather, there is symmetry. Instead of a perpetual oscillation from one to the other, between them there is a reciprocal anticipation. "Nature," wrote Pascal, "diversifies and imitates; artifice imi-

---

11. Sergio Cotta, "Le role du juriste dans la société en transformation," *Analyse et Prévision* 3 (1967): 284.
12. Emmanuel Mounier, quoted by Manaranche, p. 143.
13. Cf. Michel Foucault, *Les Mots et les choses* (Gallimard, Paris, 1966) p. 76.
14. Kostas Papaioannou, "Regnum Hominis, note sur le subjectivisme moderne," *Diogène* 41 (1963): 46–50.

tates and diversifies."[15] Far from being a robot, artificial man is the man who makes himself—as Saint Thomas noted. If he seems today to be a machine operator, this is very simply because it is at such a level that the battle for the human is now being waged. In any event, the machine as such cannot condemn man. The machine on its own could no more eliminate man than the body could silence the man who cries out: "Who will deliver me from the body of this death?" (Rom. 7:24).

Moreover, the man who makes himself is not his own maker, but a creature. From this viewpoint, if there is one mirror in which we ought to contemplate artificial man, it is that of creation and not that of nature. Artificial man can only put into relief the very notion of a creature made in the image of an imageless God, and can only help us grasp what is new in the very idea of creation as iconoclasm of nature, an iconoclasm whose intention is precisely to render to nature its nature. As the image of creation, artificial man serves to put into relief the very notion of resurrection whose intention consists in rendering to man his body, in engrafting him to it as the believer is engrafted to the body of Christ. The idea of artificial man, finally, puts into relief the very notion of a vivifying spirit: man is man only insofar as he is new man.

Man is situated between nature and artifice as between two infinities. At once sinful and justified, he is that which he is not, he is not that which he is. Neither wholly in nature, nor wholly in artifice, he must surpass himself regardless of the technique utilized or the utopianism with which it is programmed: nature, history, or technology.

But utopia is not the kingdom. Utopia is to the kingdom as nature is to creation, or as history is to redemption, or, simply, as the flesh is to the spirit. If there is a relationship between them, it is one of radical otherness, the same the apostle Paul describes when he declares: "So it is with the resurrection of the dead. What is sown is perishable, what is raised is imperishable. It is sown in dishonor, it is raised in glory. It is sown in weak-

---

15. Pascal, *Pensées*, 27. 120.

ness, it is raised in power. It is sown a physical body, it is raised a spiritual body" (1 Cor. 15:42–44).

B. The Structures of the Church

Let us move now to the second condition: the necessity for the church to remodel its structures according to the structures of technological society.

In the first place, it is important to recall what we may consider a fundamental principle: technology does not eliminate man but endows him with new dimensions. More precisely, it is not man that technology eliminates, but the individualistic understanding of the human—a notion we must replace with the communal understanding of the human. Not that technology replaces man with the group or the collectivity. Thus, for example, to the extent that, technology notwithstanding, housing developments tend to crush man, they are and remain an insult to the communal notion of the human.

Nor has the church ever advocated collectivism, much less individualism. As parish it has, on the contrary, insisted on its desire to assimilate itself to the geography of the social body by deliberately taking on the aspect of the village or the neighborhood. This is as true of Protestantism as it is of Catholicism, even if the former enjoys mixing the two notions (less geographic than political) of civil community and Christian community. In both cases, the liturgy, considered as a concrete expression of the eschatic logic of faith, serves as a hinge between the parish and the village or between the civil community and the Christian community. And if, in the former, nature in the innermost part of its substance is organized as the sacrament of grace, in the latter, political authority is arranged in terms of the word, of which it is only one of the coordinates, the other being the pastoral authority of the church.[16] In both instances, in no way do we leave the eschatological realm of liturgy, aside from the internal difference that liturgy asserts its own utopianism by

16. Cf. the Calvinist doctrine of the magistrate as minister of the word and vicar of Christ.

asserting the utopianism of nature in one instance, and that of history in the other. In one case, it mediates a geography of grace, in the other a politics of faith.

In the second place, although we must limit our scope if only because we cannot here discuss the problem in detail, it is nonetheless important to present concrete suggestions aimed at nudging the church into the framework of technological civilization.

To this end, the three conditions to which the structures of the church must respond reflect the three traits which the church assumes as people of God, as body of Christ, and as hope of the world and prolepsis of the kingdom. To consider the church as people of God is to deal with the notion of the church *day by day*. The church must be there when the manna falls from heaven: it knows that the manna falls each day and for each day sufficient is the evil thereof. Considering it as body of Christ, we are dealing with the notion of the church for today. Either the church is contemporary to the world or it is not the church, the *avant-garde* of the world. And, accordingly, considering it as hope of the world and prolepsis of the kingdom, we appeal to the notion of the church *for every day*. Since we are ultimately dealing with a church for the world of technology, these three conditions, these three aspects take account, in particular, of the fact that in the empirical realm of things, neither the geographical division of the parish, nor the sociological division of the Christian community is today spared the ax which cuts through the human or social structures once believed to be permanent.

However, some indication must now be given of what constitutes structures bearing the marks corresponding to each of those three conditions of the church:

1. Considered as people of God, the church is a day-by-day church, as daily as bread and wine. Reflecting this kind of experience, everyday language takes on expressions such as ecclesial community, grassroots community, etc. This is undoubtedly something quite different from a simple attempt to modernize jargon inherited from the Bible. And indeed it becomes especially obvious when, apart from any ideological consideration of the political commitments thus sanctioned, we observe that the

139

individual (if not individualistic) conception of pastoral or priestly ministry is disappearing and giving way to a communal conception (which must not be confused with collectivism which more often than not resonates as sheer stereophonic individualism). Of course it remains to be seen, but there should be no reason for surprise if the shift toward the priestly team were to prove an anticipation of the very notion of man as community of the human which is emerging under the pressure of technological civilization.

2. These are only infinitesimal steps in the direction of an ecclesial community whose own structures mesh with those of technological society; for the church, the body of Christ, is for today if it is a church of today. From among the many steps still to be taken in order to create a church of today, we can designate two. On the one hand, the solitary or, rather, individual exercise of the priesthood was bound up with a system of classification reflected by the very structures of the church: priesthood/laity, religious/secular, grace/nature, etc. When the functions of pastor and magistrate are combined, they reflect the movement from a society whose model is class-ridden to a society in which labor is divided and responsibilities are correlative: the universal priesthood (or authentic collegiality). But technological society is no longer characterized by diversity (as some priestly teams seem to think as they proceed, in fact, to chop up the work among themselves); what characterizes technological society is its complexity, a process of complexification which basically aims at inaugurating an understanding of man as communal form of the human. It is therefore not enough for the priestly team to be diversified, it must also become more complex; and this complexification must itself be defined according to the nature of specific tasks to be accomplished, according to the criteria of precise objectives to be reached. Then the priestly team has necessarily to be modified according to the process of complexification which permits the ecclesial community to be a grassroots community as well as the *avant-garde* of the civic community.

Furthermore, since the ecclesial community would come into being because of this or that objective which it would have set for itself, it would be normal not only for the priestly team to adjust its composition but also for specialists other than pastoral ministers to be part of it as well: engineers, judges, doctors, researchers, masons, plumbers, etc., depending on the circumstances. For what indeed is the church, the body of Christ, if not the concrete hope of the people of God, a people always on the move, always up to date?

3. Finally, a church for every day is a church whose liturgical involvement in the world consists, on the one hand, in the manifestation of the body of Christ as prolepsis of the reign of God and, on the other hand, in the manifestation of man as communal form of the human. It follows that the functions of the church can no longer be defined on the basis of some natural sacralism or some historical messianism. Quite the opposite: as future of the world, the church must define itself in terms of the missions, projects, and objectives it will have to assume in order to insert itself into the process of techno-social complexification. Cathedrals need not be made of stone. The church is not recognized by its cathedrals but by its liturgy, by its participation in a communal technique of the human. To be sure—and every cathedral still testifies to this—technology, even as the communal technique of the human, ends where living man begins: "The first man was from the earth, a man of dust: the second man is from heaven. As was the man of dust, so are those who are of heaven. Just as we have borne the image of the man of dust, we shall also bear the image of the man of heaven. . . . When the perishable puts on the imperishable, and the mortal puts on immortality, then shall come to pass the saying that is written: 'Death is swallowed up in victory'" (1 Cor. 15:47–48, 54).

Faith, said Kierkegaard, begins where reason ends. Wherever nature comes to an end, there creation can begin. And redemption begins whenever history has reached an end.

Created in the image of God, man begins where all techniques of the human leave off, where they can only go "too far" —whenever they go anywhere; where, for want of the kingdom, utopia ends. Indeed, I have stressed the importance of the facts that utopia is not defined in terms of the unrealizable, and that it matters little that this unrealizable should haunt man's quest whether through asceticism or through eroticism. But, on the other hand, if utopia is defined in terms of the realizable, this "realizable" is one that is realized on condition that utopia come to end. Nor is this realizable the end itself of utopia: it is what puts an end to utopia, it is the *eschaton,* that is to say, that of which the new man is the event. For the reign of God to take place, it is in no way necessary that man reach his goal or that all his possibilities be realized. It is enough that God alone is all in all, in view of which he is and remains the radically other, the one of whom man is the condition.

Who is this man? Again, he remains to be realized, since he is the man in whose body everyone with an engrafted heart participates: the man who no longer belongs to himself, having passed from death to life and for whom Christ is life.

But in Christ, the end of the Law and consequently the end of all utopias, there is no man of nature, nor of history, nor of technique, any more than there is Jew or Greek, man or woman, freedman or slave. "For as in one body we have many members, and all the members do not have the same function, we, though many, are one body in Christ, and individually members one of another. Having gifts that differ according to the grace given to us . . ." (Rom. 12:4–6).

Landmark or obstacle, sign or impediment, symbol or barrier, the role of the church is bound to be what is at stake between utopia and the kingdom.

3. CHRIST: HUMANITY OF GOD
AND REALITY OF MAN

As the saying goes, man is born either a Platonist or an Aristotelian. Similarly, once the stage of intellectual weaning was reached, a choice had to be made between theism and atheism. Although usually dualistic, it sometimes happened that theism became tinged with monism and, conversely, that atheism, usually monistic, became tinged with dualism. In any event, dualism ultimately managed to get the upper hand over theism, a fact that can easily be established through a simple cultural analysis of the death of God. Moreover, the prey was more interesting than the predator, as is revealed in the fact that the collapse of theism brought with it that of atheism. And it is, consequently, in his innermost self that man is aching, for he cannot live by immanence alone.

That is, indeed, the reason man is claimed to be the transcendence of man. But then the inevitable question arises: What will prevent such a transcendence from being crushed by monism in the same way as theism was crushed by dualism?

Nor can the problem of God be indefinitely postponed with impunity, any more than it can be solved allegedly by reducing God to anonymity (monism), or even by encumbering him with pseudonyms (dualism). In other words, we must neither over-name him, as dualism tends to do, nor under-name him, under-identify him, as monism seems inclined to do. Still, we must name him. And, unless we have allowed ourselves to be misled, we cannot evade the affirmation to which our argument has been leading: the naming of God belongs to the realm of eschatology, is in fact the eschatic word par excellence.

In another context, this affirmation would, of course, have called for a more detailed discussion. But in the present case two kinds of indications will bring the sufficient confirmation we need. The first deals with the trinitarian notion of God and the second with the humanity of God, that is to say, with the Christology of man.

First of all, the trinitarian doctrine is nothing but the Christian response to the question which neither dualism nor monism, in their antagonism, succeeds in resolving. Unfortunately, in order to express this response which we have qualified as Christian it was formerly necessary to call upon a language and upon categories of thought forged either by dualism or, less often, by monism. Hence both gnosis and speculation, respectively, were invoked.

More precisely, in order to name God, Christian thought fell back either upon a utopianism of the soul or upon a utopianism of the spirit, resorting at one point to a utopianism based on an evasion by way of the soul which aspires to a primal union with God, at another point to a utopianism based on a flight forward by the spirit which aspires to final communion with God. Thus, quite appropriately, Rosemary Ruether has pointed out that utopia exhales a certain ascetic odor.[17] This is true enough, but with the reservation that we restrict ourselves to the classical utopianisms of the soul with their supernatural tendencies or to those of the spirit with their messianic tendencies. Besides, it is not entirely because of their propensity for asceticism that these kinds of utopia create a problem. They are a problem simply because they confirm the bifurcation of man, break the fundamental unity of body and soul, of flesh and spirit. This is true of monism, which tries to deny these dichotomies by collapsing one of the terms into the other, and it is equally true of dualism, which uses one term to neutralize the other. In the first case, the relation between man and God is a relation of identity; in the second, it is one of difference. Accordingly, either man is absorbed into God, or God is wholly expelled; or, alternately, God is either absorbed into man or reduces man to nothing. In this way God and man are transformed into denominators of one another. What they miss, in each case, is the *name* that allows the one to take place through the other without, however, reducing them both to a common denominator.

Thus, in the biblical tradition, God is more ineffable than he is unnameable. He names himself by giving a name to the man who has no name, by calling "my people" those that are not his people. He names himself, but only through that which does not localize him. He takes place only in naming himself, in revealing himself as wholly other, the radically other closer to man than man is to himself.

Therefore, according to the parable of the Good Samaritan (Luke 10:25–37), to name someone means to acknowledge the other as neighbor. Likewise, it is only in speaking of the otherness of God that we can name him.

In contrast to the utopianisms of soul and spirit, the trinitarian understanding of God, in which is reflected the eschatic logic of faith, endeavors to maintain this relation of otherness. God does not create as does a demiurge. God does noth-

---

17. Rosemary Ruether, *The Radical Kingdom* (Harper & Row, New York, 1970), p. 13.

ing without letting man do what he does. If God's word is incarnate, it is because man can take it upon himself to speak; God speaks by letting man speak. Finally, as spirit, God gives life to man and, since he himself is the living one, he lets man live.

So it follows that an anthropological utopianism which consists in the eschatic logic of faith, and which is proper to the new man, corresponds to this theological utopianism proper to the trinitarian approach. But for the new man, Christ is life, and to know the benefits of Christ is to know God, to name him. Thus the relation of otherness is established, without which God is nothing more than what man is not, without which man is neither the condition of God the radically other nor the event of God. Yet, it is precisely this event which is the resurrection of Christ and, through it, the resurrection of man as body, as member of the body of Christ.

4. THE CHURCH:
BODY OF CHRIST AND PLEROMA

The problem of the church is like the problem of God. For a long time, Christianity was content to conceive of God as a universal hypothesis, a principle of explanation. Because of this, theology continually ran the risk of betraying its own task and allowing itself to turn into theodicy, rather than a critique of it. Better still, theology is indeed nothing less than a critique of the idea of God.

Moreover, how could it have been otherwise if in order to speak of God (*von Gott*, in Bultmann's terms), in fact, we cannot do any better than speak about God (*über Gott*)?[18] And yet theology is a critique of the idea of God only to the extent that by God is understood the critique of this critical theology. Other-

---

18. Bultmann, *Faith and Understanding*, I, pp. 53, 64. Cf. René Marlé, "Parler de Dieu selon R. Bultmann et G. Ebeling," in *L'analyse du langage théologique,* ed. Enrico Castelli (Aubier, Paris, 1969).

wise, how could God not be confused with the idol which, as Maritain puts it, can be god but is never quite God. Furthermore, this critique of the critical idea of God must necessarily be developed from a concrete base, the church: a base so concrete and demanding, so visible and ambiguous, that (out of a sense of embarrassment, one likes to think) both exigency and ambiguity had to be justified by invoking an invisible church. And the problem of the church came to be treated in the same way as the problem of God. Nonetheless, if our claim concerning the problem of God is not without basis, it follows that the Christian faith, like theology, has no hermeneutical principle other than the church. At the very least, it follows that the hermeneutic of the Christian faith is an ecclesial, that is to say eschatological, hermeneutic[19] since the church is the communal form of the *eschaton*.

Let me try to express this more clearly.

1. The church is the scriptural form of the word of God and, also, it is the verbal form of the scriptures. As we know all too well, Catholics and Protestants have differed as to whether tradition had priority over scriptures or, on the contrary, scriptures alone had complete authority. Opting for the first solution, Catholics relied on the magisterium of the church while Protestants, opting for the second, relied on the magisterium of the word alone. The problem could thus be reduced to a mere variation on the riddle of the chicken and the egg. The fact remains, however, that on the Catholic as well as on the Protestant side scriptures had no status apart from that of received texts, of *scripta*. And what is more, since this status was itself confirmed by the closing of the canon, revelation at the same time found itself trapped in the ephemeral structures of a particular cultural phenomenon of which the Bible, all things considered, was the ultimate sedimentation. The believer had only two resources: to proceed with the retrieval of the word of God contained in

---

19. Hermeneutic comes from a Greek word meaning interpretation, which we take in the sense of a play which would be no play were it not for the interpretation of the various actors.

scriptures by considering the church *either* as the culmination of such an undertaking *or* as its preliminary condition. However, in both cases the church could only manifest the visible face of a hidden reality, invisible as well as Platonic, somewhere between memory and hope, between the *already* of grace and the *not yet* of salvation.

Surely, our motive for rejecting this way of posing the question is obvious. The eschatic logic of faith is compromised on the Catholic as well as on the Protestant side. It is compromised by virtue of the hiatus introduced at the outset between scriptures and the church, a hiatus whose repercussions are bound to affect at once the relation between the church and society, faith and the world. Though inaugurated by the coming of Christ, the fulfillment of scriptures nonetheless remains suspended until the end of time.

In Christ's own words, however, it is here and now that all is fulfilled: that is to say, there are no scriptures other than those through which the word of God is fulfilled. And of this word the church is the scriptural form, its reproduction. But the church is also the verbal form of the scriptures, for there are no scriptures apart from their production through the church. That is why we can adopt even rather traditional formulas according to which the church is correctly conceived at once as mother of the faith and its trustee. Matrix of the faith to the extent that she is its trust, trustee of the faith to the extent that she is its mother, the church manifests itself as both the verbal form of scriptures and the scriptural form of the word of God. For this reason, the church represents the *eschaton,* in its communal form.

2. As communal form of the *eschaton,* the church cannot be reduced to a particular form of community.

Particular forms of community are those which are called, for example, Israel, the Roman Catholic Church, the Reformed Church of France. In the New Testament the term church designates both the two or three who gather together in the name of Christ and any local church or the church as a whole, the people of God. It designates the body of Christ in full operation, in exercise, as if each of its functions

147

emerged, not from a single ecclesiology, but from a diversity, a plurality of ecclesiologies,[20] even, we would like to say, from an ecclesiology in process of complexification. In a word, church designates not so much a communal pluralism as that which gives human form to communal diversification. And in this sense the church is more communion than community.

As Yves Congar points out, during the reign of Pepin the Short and especially under Charlemagne, the term church in practice designates both the empire and the church proper, both society and the body of Christ. A principle of communion, the church was thus identified with a particular form of community. Faced with this danger, Pope Gregory VII sought to free the church from lay power. The result was the separation of the church and the world, a separation which the institutionalization of the church would later consolidate. Fearful, not perhaps without reason, that its freedom would be threatened by the identification of the body of Christ with the empire, that it would be compromised by what Barth called the flight into the visible,[21] the church reacted; and this is to be expected. Unfortunately, it is not always perceived soon enough that with such a reaction the church runs the risk of a flight into the invisible or, more exactly, a flight away from the visible, as if it were not in the world that faith must come into play, but only in the framework of the church.

It does not follow, however, that the church should situate itself somewhere between those two extremes. The problem arises precisely from the fact that in reality they are not extremes at all, at least from the point of view of faith as eschatic existence; they are merely the concrete form assumed by the twofold exigency to which the new man submits, the man for whom believing in God necessarily implies an equally radical involvement in the world, and for whom the church must guard against assimilating itself to the world as well as against alienating itself from it.

---

20. Cf. Hartwig Thyen, "Zur Problematik einer Neutestamentlichen Ekklesiologie," in *Frieden-Bibel-Kirche*, ed. Gerhard Liedke (Ernst Klett Verlag, Stuttgart/Kösel-Verlag, Munich, 1972), pp. 96 ff.
21. Karl Barth, *L'Eglise* (Labor et Fides, Geneva, 1964), p. 35.

It is therefore not surprising that, in the primitive church, it certainly is not through the liturgy that the community of the faithful ever provides itself with structures which would separate it from the community of men.[22] As we have already said, if there had been a social mold peculiar to the church, faith would thereby have been reduced to an ideology. The church is neither another world nor anything other than the world; it is an *other* world, that which is changed by the coming of the reign of God.

3. As communal form of the *eschaton,* that is neither more nor less than the future of God in the world, the church *has* no future, it *is* the future.

With this paradoxical formula we simply want to emphasize that from the New Testament point of view the church does not end with the end of the world but with the "return of Christ." It is in this sense that the church has no end, or rather that it is indefectible.

To witness to the fact that God alone can be all in all, there is no need for the church to wait for the end of the world—the world would have to disappear before the reign of God could happen, and man would have to be obliterated for the reality of God to appear. On the contrary, the church belongs in the world[23] as though in a foreign country,[24] since it belongs to God as well. Conversely, the world is never so foreign a place that the church cannot adopt its structures. Indeed, how could the church scorn the world if the church must make of it a world which God so loves that he gives his only son to it (John 3:16)? But it is here, in this gift of God, and nowhere else, that the end of the world takes place; it is here that the reign of God takes place, putting an end to all the futurisms in which the world revels or by which it is sobered up; and here God makes a new world.

The second reason why the church has no future has to do with the affinities between an eschatological conception of the

---

22. Cf. Eduard Schweizer, *The Church as the Body of Christ* (John Knox Press, Atlanta, 1964), p. 33.
23. Karl Ludwig Schmidt, "Eglise," *Dictionnaire biblique* (Labor et Fides, Geneva, n.d.), p. 109.
24. The etymology of the word "parish" means nothing different.

church and technological utopianism. Technological utopianism, in this respect, is accused of having no ends. But should we not rather be glad about this? Far from eliminating man's responsibility, technology, since it has no ends, renders that responsibility all the more urgent. Besides, there has never been a more harmful impediment to the promotion of the human than man himself *(homo homini lupus)*. The parable of the Last Judgment (Matt. 25) is a marvelous illustration of this: access to the kingdom is barred precisely to those who have not, mechanically, given food to those who were hungry and drink to those who were thirsty, without bothering to inquire whether or not this earned them the kingdom. The reason for this is, in a sense, that the promotion of the human is too important a responsibility to be entrusted exclusively to man. No one is more capable than he is of thwarting it. Doubtless, today man is more capable than ever of frustrating the human, of obliterating man. But that we can still speak about it is enough to show that in the final analysis, this is a matter of an impossible possibility, and that, in any case, it is not illusory to hope that man remains to be realized, however little he believes in God.

Here, very simply, are the results of two thousand years of Christianity. They are not meager. It is important to recall them, if only to show that an ecclesial revolution is still a possibility today. Of course, for this to happen, Christianity must be endowed with an ecclesiology that does not scorn the technological world; it must be endowed with the ecclesiology needed to cross the threshold of technological society.

On the threshold of technological society, it remains only for us to draw from the past the lessons which will permit us to cope with the future of the church. If, to this end, we must begin by designating the two important moments prior to technological civilization which have marked the structures of the church in terms of contemporary social realities, we ought immediately to call to mind, first, an ecclesiology with priestly overtones and, second, an ecclesiology with prophetic overtones.

In the service of a society still set in the mold of the sacred, an ecclesiology with sacerdotal overtones is the translation, on the temporal as well as the spiritual plane, of the ascetic utopianism which is characteristic of a social reality whose life is

150

punctuated by the rhythm of the supernatural cycle, with its various sacraments mediating the reign of God throughout the earth. The main temptation of such an ecclesiology is obviously an acculturation to sacrality, that is to say, the confinement of the church in the womb of the sacral universe and the identification of the church with the structures of the corresponding society.

But the medieval church is not the only one to imprison itself in its own ecclesiology. The same thing happens to an ecclesiology with prophetic overtones—which is the translation, on the civil as well as the religious plane, of a utopianism whose aspirations belong to the realm of ethics rather than of asceticism. One can already feel that here money has taken over from the sacred; and in order to desacralize it Calvin does not hesitate to abrogate the condemnation laid on usury by the whole Middle Ages. We no longer work as we pray. *Homo orans* of the middle ages has given way to *homo laborans* of the Modern Age, the man who can only pray as he works, work being for him a form of prayer. The liturgy of the kingdom changes its site: it is no longer otherworldliness which inspires man, but rather a new world where secular tasks are as fascinating as the call of the sacred once was. Under these conditions, it is obvious that acculturation to secularism will constitute the main temptation of a prophetic ecclesiology. Words end up sounding empty when they no longer come to terms with the reality they designate, and ethics ends up describing a system of customs and conventions.

We venture an observation here which will undoubtedly appear unjust: these two ecclesiologies are both ultimately totalitarian; they both echo, in some way, conceptions which are unitary in relation to the social organization of common life. One king, one law, one faith; *cuius regio eius religio:* as goes the law and the king, so goes the faith. Now, the unity of the church has never been, or should never have been, more than an article of faith. It is not the condition of the (good) visibility of the church, but the expression of this visibility that is at stake in the ecclesial complexification of faith confronting the pluralism of human communities.

Apart from the fact that an ecclesial revolution can never be a totalitarian revolution, it is more than ever necessary to re-place the totalitarian conception of the church with a pleromatic ecclesiology. For the "figure," the symbol, of the reign of God does not consist in a cosmos, a totality enmeshed in its own structures, but in a pleroma, a fullness in which flesh and spirit are knit together, as are God and man when God is all in all.

It is nonetheless true that an ecclesiology with pleromatic overtones, which is the only ecclesiology able both to confront the syncretistic pluralism of a technological civilization and to adopt the framework of understanding proper to technological utopianism, is not necessarily free of all obstacles. These obsta-cles are not derived from technological utopianism itself, at least not directly. They are due in particular to the twofold acculturation in which the Christian faith seems locked up. This means that Christians, whatever their confession, are still them-selves prisoners of the past, hostages of the Constantinian civili-zation.

As everyone knows, today it is simply through *cultural* atavism that one is Protestant or Catholic. In the wake of the death of God, this is the very least that Christians of various confessions ought to admit. Sometimes, they even do so. Consequently, the Catholic church still believes itself to be the sole keeper of the true ecumenicity of faith, while the World Council of Churches conceives the unity of faith according to a model of catholicity no less Roman. Yet, the true catholicity of the church is recog-nized by one sign and one sign alone: namely, that this earth *(terre)* is but a *pied-à-terre* for the church (Heb. 11:8–10). And, likewise, the true ecumenicity of the church is also recognized by a single sign: namely, that nothing human is alien to the church. Indeed, the human consists in humanizing that which is not human, and above all man himself; it consists in humaniz-ing all that which, because it is alien to man, would try to annihilate the human and frustrate its reign.

To be sure, all this is well known on both sides of the confes-sional barrier. To wit, never have the manifestations of a Chris-tianity gone wild been surrounded with so much solicitude, and never have they been the object of such complicity, even while they are timidly disavowed. All this permits the church to coddle its deficiencies and, above all, to avoid tackling head-on the challenge of technological civilization.

Let us speak about this challenge. Contrary to popular belief, it consists neither in biology nor in cybernetics. It is a religious challenge. Certainly, it is not a challenge to religion. But insofar as this religious challenge is presented by a technological civilization, it is at once simpler and more serious. It is a challenge put forth in the name of a technological revolution which is at the same time a religious revolution. Marked, at least for the moment, by a syncretistic orientation, technological religiosity appears far less inclined toward sacramental contemplation or prophetic involvement than toward some gratuitous dionysiacs of the body or, for that matter, of the spirit. It is experiential, not in the sense of a conversion of man to God, but in the sense of a reciprocal inversion of God and man.

It is in view of the thoroughly religious character of this challenge put forth by technological civilization that we have advanced the idea of an ecclesiology with pleromatic or, if one prefers, charismatic overtones. What are its characteristics?

To put it simply, if, from the perspective of a sacerdotal ecclesiology all is sacred, and from the perspective of a prophetic ecclesiology all is vocation, then from the perspective of a pleromatic or charismatic ecclesiology, what must be stressed, in view of technological efficiency, is its gratuitousness: in other words, the fact that all is grace.[25]

As communal form of the *eschaton,* the church *(ecclesia),* the people of God, is a people of grace. The pre-established harmony of the cosmos is replaced here by the idea of a God who is all in all because he is and remains the radically other: pleroma and totality are not confused.

Out of this relation of otherness between God and man issues the iconoclastic character of the church as principle of social novation. Because God is spirit, the temple must be destroyed, for the church is church only to the extent that it is in commu-

---

25. Let us recall the pastor in Bernanos' *The Diary of a Country Priest* (and Bernanos only repeats Theresa of Lisieux here): dying outside of a church, enclosed in the past, he receives the last rites at the hands of a defrocked priest and says, "all is grace."

nion with the social reality of communal forms of the human. To be part of the church means less to participate in a community than to be in communion with others, than to become all things to all men *(koinonia),* as Saint Paul puts it (1 Cor. 9:22).

Finally, to the extent that the church is the body of Christ, it is the scriptural form of the word become flesh, and asserts the world as means of grace. It is lordly *(kyriakos).* Only on this condition can we still say today, with Saint Augustine, that no one can believe in the Gospel unless compelled by the charismatic authority of the church.

Technological utopianism is no more centered on the beginning of beginnings or on the end of ends than is the eschatic logic of faith. Technological utopianism is focused neither on the past nor on the future, but on the present, on the time of the human, the only time with which God could be contemporary, the only time attuned to the fullness of time, pleroma of the God who comes.